PLEASE TAKE ONE*

*ONE STEP TOWARDS A MORE GENEROUS LIFE

Mike Dickson

THE GENEROUS PRESS

PLEASE TAKE ONE*

*ONE STEP TOWARDS A MORE GENEROUS LIFE

First published in Great Britain in 2010 by
The Generous Press, 59A Portobello Road,
London W11 3DB

This edition published 2010
© Michael Dickson, 2010
mikedickson@pleasetakeonestep.com
www.pleasetakeonestep.com
www.themoreyougive.co.uk

Printed in the UK by Cox & Wyman Ltd, Reading
Cover and marketing by Profero
Interior design Henry Iles
ISBN: 978-0-9551591-2-1

For Shuna, Annabel and William
with love and thanks

Thank you

'From quiet homes and first beginning, out to the undiscovered ends, there's nothing worth the wear of winning but laughter and the love of friends'

Hilaire Belloc

It wouldn't have been possible to write any of this book without the input, encouragement and generosity of a wonderful and varied group of people, most of whom have patiently listened to me twitter (in the original meaning of the word) on about 'The Book' for far too long. To all those friends, 'encouragers' and helpers who gave me their time, introduced me to interesting sources and people, told me their stories, read draft copies, and at all times were patient, clever, kind – and incredibly generous – thanks so much: you are all stars!

Alba and Prabhakar Goswami; Amir Amirani; Annabel and William; Anne Cowley; Annie Foster; Arti; Benny Refson; Bruno Guissani; Charles and Elizabeth Handy; Charles Gurassa; Charlie Fraser; Chipo Chung; Clare Townhill; David and Tina Griffith; David Gold; Elizabeth and Rory Brooks; Elspeth Lynn; Erin; Eugenie Harvey; Franny Armstrong; Henry Iles; Hugh Homan; Jean and Graham Ross Russell; John Fisher; John Morgan; Kerry Ten Kate; Laura Fraser; Lizzie Gillett; Liz Mayhew; Matt Kepple; Max Kennedy; Michael Johnson; Michael Norton; Nicole Seagrim; Olly Donnelly; Paul Hogarth; Pete Yeo; Rabbi Joseph Edelheit; Rev Mark Hargreaves; Robert Holden; Rowan Lawton; Sarah Fairburn; Sarah Kuenhe; Sat Swarley; Selina Mills; Shuna; Susannah Steel; Thiywe Khumalo; Tony Juniper; Vince Gwilliam; Dr Vincent Pattison; and Wendy Tracey

And Profero www.profero.com

And the people at Ted www.ted.com

And Google.

Contents

Preface 1

Introduction 5

1. The Age of I 9

2. Generosity 19

3. Happiness 39

4. Enough 51

5. Poverty in Britain 79

6. Generosity at home 103

7. Generous communities 119

8. Global poverty 137

9. The environment 161

10. My Generous Life 187

Resources 203

The Author 216

Preface

Whatever you can do, or dream you can do, begin it now. Boldness has genius, power and magic in it, begin it now.

GOETHE

If I can do it, anyone can

'Who's up for running the London Marathon?'

It was 1988 and I was at a Christmas party. Our host had managed to get hold of twelve entries for the race from one of the sponsors.

Feeling very much at peace with the world after several glasses of wine, I put my hand up to run. Then I went home and enthusiastically called an equally non-athletic friend, Ricky, a senior paediatrician at Great Ormond Street hospital, persuading him to join me in my latest adventure.

I started training. Slowly.

The weeks passed. As race day drew closer I decided that if I was going to go through all this pain and suffering I might as well do it for something worthwhile. Like many others I was vaguely aware of the world of charities, had even thought that it would be good to support one, but had never actually got round to it. I remembered then something that had happened a few years previously.

A young girl in a powered wheelchair had driven into the shop I owned in Covent Garden. She pressed a control that raised her seat until she was the same height as the counter, bought an item, lowered the seat, then sped out into the piazza. I had been intrigued enough to remember the name of the manufacturers and now I called them, to discover that each wheelchair cost £3,500.

I asked if they had any children on their waiting list. They mentioned a girl called Sammy, who had cerebral palsy and lived in Lincoln. As much to give myself courage and inspiration for the marathon ahead as anything else, I cleared a day from my diary, got on a train and went to meet her.

Sammy and her grandmother met me at the station and took me home to tea. I had never met a disabled child and I had no idea what cerebral palsy was. I spent about two hours talking to them both and was profoundly moved. Sammy was very bright, but had trouble with her speech and was unable to move much without help from her granny or a friend. I asked Sammy for a picture of herself and returned to London, where I reported back to Ricky. We agreed to run for Sammy, to buy her a powered wheelchair. We sent begging letters to all our friends with a picture of Sammy and the message: 'We are going to do something daft and mildly heroic; run 26.2 miles to help a young girl, who can't move about independently, get out of her front door on her own.'

By the day of the London Marathon neither of us had run more than six miles, but we had raised over £9,000, an extraordinary sum in those days. Some people even sponsored us to cross the starting line! Ricky, who had been expressly told by his doctor not to run because of a medical condition but had got himself signed off as fit anyway, put a large X on his number (to identify himself to First Aid stations) and strapped some pills to his wrist. We hugged each other and set off into the unknown, with almost no idea of what we were doing. We knew it was going to be a challenge but, we reasoned, we had all day to reach the finish. Six hours and thirty minutes later, when all the traffic separation schemes had been removed, I staggered across the finishing line! Ricky had made it in a more respectable five hours. Our mission had been accomplished. We headed home for a hot bath, and then out for a great celebratory dinner with our wives, overjoyed and knackered and proudly wearing our medals.

In April 1990, just one year after the London Marathon, we registered Whizz-Kidz as a charity. Since then it has raised over £50 million, provided mobility equipment for more than seven thousand disabled children and helped thousands of others. It has become well-respected throughout the UK and is the largest supplier of paediatric mobility aids outside the National Health Service.

A life-changing event

The improvement in mobility helped to make Sammy's life a little better – and it completely changed mine. I discovered a great deal about how charities work, and gradually awakened from my own small, self-obsessed world. I began to learn first-hand about the impact and rewards of 'giving'. I realised that people who give generously, who go out of their way to help others, often get back as much as they give. I noticed that when many of the fundraisers met a disabled young person, often the child for whom they had raised money, the impact on them was enormous. They were both moved and humbled that their fundraising efforts had helped a child who was unable to move, move. To become independently mobile, to 'whizz' about on their own, go shopping, go to a decent school, play with friends, take part in sport. Not infrequently these people confided in me that helping a child move had been the best thing they had done in the year.

I too was amazed and humbled. By the optimism and spirit of the disabled children I met, and by the amazing families who looked after them with such astonishing patience and love. By the care and attention of those surrounding the children – the carers and physiotherapists, the occupational therapists, the manufacturers of the special mobility equipment. It was wonderful to watch and to be involved in, albeit in a very small way. I sometimes wondered whether some of these wonderful yet ordinary people were made on another planet. I discovered what an enormous privilege it is to be able to help others and how hugely rewarding it is to be able to inspire all kinds of other people to do so.

My co-founders and I simply felt very blessed, that we were the right people in the right place at the right time. True serendipity.

But my main reason for including a little of my story in this book is to encourage everyone to go for it. If a forty-year-old man with absolutely no running experience – not much experience of any form of exercise, in fact – can survive a marathon and with a couple of friends start a successful charity for disabled children, with absolutely no knowledge about charities, and even less about disability; well frankly there is hope for everyone!

Introduction

Time to change the world

'You must be the change you wish to see in the world'

MAHATMA GANDHI

For the last thirty years, most of us in the western world have been having a party. We have been encouraged to be self-sufficient and independent. To become successful, rich, search for true happiness, and find 'the real us'. To buy our own homes, invest in shares, become entrepreneurs, travel the world and borrow as much money as we liked to consume 'things' that upon cool, calm reflection we didn't really need. Or use. We have been cleverly and ruthlessly advertised and marketed at to buy a lifestyle rather than get a real life. We thought we had it all.

But now, the world is not in a happy state. And neither are most of us. We are nationally, corporately and individually bust. Owing unimaginable trillions that would make our own more prudent forebears groan with disbelief, and which will take our children decades to repay.

I think it is time to change the world. For every one of us

to wake up and decide that we, ourselves, can tackle the challenges our society faces, as individuals and in groups. We all can become leaders and authors of change, by living more generous, proactive lives, by inspiring each other and by setting an example to our friends and to our children.

We know in our hearts that it is good to be generous. Each one of us feels far better about ourselves when we can help other people, and we are touched when others are generous to us. A generous life is a life well lived, and a happier life. The challenge is to find a way to lead a more generous life in the real world.

As individuals we cannot hope to address the problems we and the world face – socially, economically and environmentally – but collectively we can. It is time to be more generous and to build a more generous world; a world not of you and me, but you or me. To recapture some of the practical simplicity of the ways that we used to live, when we were dependent on each other. To set out to create a world, rather than acquire one. To take the first step towards a more generous life.

Make the world a better place

Generosity isn't about money, though giving money to a good cause or even a person – quietly and without ceremony – can be an important element in a life worth living. Giving of ourselves is the greatest act of generosity.

A generous life involves putting more effort into looking after each other; becoming actively involved with our own communities; speaking up for the poorest and most disadvantaged members of our society and becoming their champions and ambassadors; paying attention to the plight of the world's poorest people and learning how we can help them; actively campaigning to save our planet; amassing fewer things that we don't really need and withdrawing our financial support from those who are destroying our world for purely commercial gain. It involves acknowledging that we do care about the destruction of the rainforest, about preserving fish in the sea and tigers on land for our children to wonder at when they are grown up. And that we value these things more than fabric conditioner.

Our society is overflowing with people whose everyday lives do indeed involve an enormous amount of love and care for others. Who do their jobs, but who are also generous with their lives. We need to cheer these people on, celebrate their work and create a mood that encourages them to emerge and to thrive. In this book you will read of extraordinary people who work tirelessly, seven days a week, to help others. But there are many more – teachers, doctors, nurses, ambulance drivers, charity workers, firemen, social workers – whose daily work includes a generosity of spirit that we should admire and applaud.

We want our children to be taught well and inspired to learn. If we are ill, our lives might depend on a student nurse or a junior doctor on their fourth night shift. A group of brave firemen might save our home, a Macmillan nurse care for our mother. They are the people on whom we truly rely. And yet it is one of the sad ironies of modern life that people often seem to be paid in inverse proportion to their value to society.

But there is hope. We live in an exciting and optimistic age where ideas, campaigns and movements can spread to millions of people instantly through the internet and social networking sites. All of us as individuals, families, schools, businesses, politicians, journalists, faith leaders – young or old – can use these outlets to spread the power of generosity and of living more generous lives; to encourage each other, tell stories from different countries and cultures, recount inspirational tales of generosity that we have experienced, and report examples of the generous acts we have done.

Because we are better than we have been, and because we can.

1. The age of I

'It was the best of times, it was the worst of times, it was the age of wisdom, it was the age of foolishness, it was the epoch of belief, it was the epoch of incredulity, it was the season of Light, it was the season of Darkness, it was the spring of hope, it was the winter of despair, we had everything before us, we had nothing before us, we were all going direct to Heaven, we were all going direct the other way'

CHARLES DICKENS, A TALE OF TWO CITIES

How did we get into this mess?

The world is not in a happy state. And neither are most of us. We have been living in The Age of I, seeking to buy a lifestyle rather than get a real life. We felt invincible.

But we were not, and nor was our world. In going for economic growth we have accumulated record levels of debt fuelled by borrowing against property prices we imagined would never stop rising and a plethora of plastic and easy credit. It has taken a financial collapse for us to realise our combined foolishness. And greed.

In February 2010 the UK government was quoted as borrowing £500 million a day. Bringing it down to an understandable perspective, this means that for every twenty teachers in a school, four are being paid for with borrowed money. Cuts in public services are inevitable; it's just a case of how much and where.

At a global level, key minerals are running out. It is estimated that, by 2040, eighty percent of the world's oil, gold, silver, mercury, lead, sulphur, tin, tungsten and zinc will have been used up. Stocks of foods are endangered too. The Japanese are stock-piling and deep freezing bluefin tuna, no doubt to sell when supplies no longer exist.

In debt nationally, corporately and individually, we need to change our behaviour and face up to a very different future. We have been pillaging the planet, consuming too many 'things' and ignoring the clear warning signals of climate change. Amid glaring inequality, great wealth still sits alongside great poverty. Global population growth is already exacerbating water and food shortages. It is impossible to overstate the huge amount at stake for future generations.

The interlinked challenges we face – managing and conserving our environment and challenging the increase of global poverty – coupled with real prospects of social breakdown, are this generation's 'World Wars'. In years to come our children will say to us 'you knew this was happening; what did you do?'

It is worth recalling the true extent of the descent into financial chaos, but not for very long. As the saying goes 'where you is, is where you is' and our urgent task now is to rebuild a more sensible and compassionate future, based upon redis-covering old values and on generosity.

SO WHO IS TO BLAME?
....

In an article in *Vanity Fair* entitled *The Great American Steal*, Bruce Feirstein listed the 'hundred people, companies, institutions and vices responsible for the economic mess' in America, 'the grand wizards of the financial apocalypse'. Prominent among them was what he called the Goldman Sachs cabal – alumni of the famous investment bank who at that time played a key part in government – along with predatory lenders (No income? No job? No problem!), the 'dark knights of banking' and 'eyes-wide-shut' regulators. All of them had a central role in the catastrophic meltdown of the US banking system. But at the end of the day, blame also lay with those 'greater fools – the infantile American consumers, who bought all those luxury SUVs and wide-screen TVs they didn't need, signed all those mortgage agreements they didn't read, lost their retirement accounts and jobs, and, in the end, paid for all the bailouts.'

....

It seems barely credible that it took only a tiny group of peo-ple, some of whom were the heads of our most respected financial institutions, to ruin those same companies, and bring about the financial calamity that has defined our age. Several 'blue chip' institutions went bust and more would have done had their governments not bailed them out. For 'the government' read us, the very ordinary man and woman in the street, going about our normal lives, admittedly whilst treating our own finances in a cavalier manner.

Collateralised debt obligations, derivatives, sub-prime mortgages, short selling – no I have no real idea what these weapons of financial mass destruction are either. More significantly, neither did 99% of those working in the financial sector at the time, including many of the heads of the investment banks who employed the people who bought and sold them. Banks and investment houses granted unimaginable bonuses to individuals, for what in effect was years spent learning how to gamble in a casino with unlimited chips.

At a meeting of the G20 in 2009, Brazilian President Luiz Inacio Lula da Silva, who had little formal education himself and had started work at the age of twelve as a shoe-shiner and street vendor, caught the mood of all the world's peoples when he said: "This was a crisis that was fostered and boosted by the irrational behaviour of people who were white-skinned and blue-eyed, who before the crisis looked like they knew everything about economics, but now have demonstrated they know nothing about economics."

With persistent and persuasive lobbying, the new masters of the universe encouraged us all to believe that they knew what they were doing; that their work was essential for the growth of western economies; and that their wealth would 'trickle down' to the rest of us. They argued that the vast amounts they earned in fees and bonuses were a mere drop in the ocean compared with their value to the country and its people. Not often was the word 'greed' mentioned. With a wave of their magic wands, and the active assistance of small armies of lawyers and accountants, most of this surreal wealth did indeed 'trickle down' – into offshore tax havens. Many of these heroes have since left the country for gentler, warmer spots where they can become 'non-doms' – tax-avoiding world citizens who can return to Britain for ninety days a year. Meanwhile the governments who bailed us all out, with our own money, are left to grapple with a truly dreadful recession.

It is hard to overestimate the structural earthquake that has hit the fabric of society in Britain. The combination of rising unemployment, falling tax revenues and the need for public spending cuts is already causing significant hardship. Many more of us will be poorer, and will need support of one kind or another. According to the UK data company Experian, the sections of society who will experience the greatest levels of financial stress include young people and pensioners, families on modest incomes, the unemployed, single parents and the long term sick. In other words, the most vulnerable people in society.

Lifestyle pornography

We must take some responsibility for our situation. It is one thing to be told that a 125% mortgage loan is ours for the asking, another thing altogether to accept it; not to think through the implications of the offer and realise it isn't our welfare that's top of the agenda here. Ditto credit cards with 26% APR – interest free for the first few months.

It is one thing to be targeted and marketed to and persuaded that debt is fine and will one day evaporate: it is quite another thing to believe it to be true.

THAT WHICH MAKES LIFE WORTHWHILE

'We will never find a purpose for our nation nor for our personal satisfaction in the mere search for economic well-being, in endlessly amassing terrestrial goods.'

'We cannot measure the national spirit on the basis of the Dow-Jones, nor can we measure the achievements of our country on the basis of the gross domestic product.'

'Our gross national product counts air pollution and cigarette advertising, and ambulances to clear our highways of carnage. It counts special locks for our doors and the jails for those who break them. It counts napalm and the cost of a nuclear warhead, and armored cars for police who fight riots in our streets. It counts Whitman's rifle and Speck's knife, and the television programs which glorify violence in order to sell toys to our children.'

'Yet the gross national product does not allow for the health of our children, the quality of their education, or the joy of their play. It does not include the beauty of our poetry or the strength of our marriages; the intelligence of our public debate or the integrity of our public officials.'

'It measures neither our wit nor our courage; neither our wisdom nor our learning; neither our compassion nor our devotion to our country; it measures everything, in short, except that which makes life worthwhile. And it tells us everything about America except why we are proud that we are Americans.'

Speech by Robert Kennedy, 18 March 1968, University of Kansas; three months before his assassination

••

Something fatuous has seeped into our daily lives – led by armies of people trying to persuade us to buy things we don't need. Pause for a moment and have a look around your home and ponder on all the stuff that lies around unused, most of which you bought with your own money when it seemed like a good idea.

We have been lulled into watching TV programmes that the Romans would have produced if they had had TV. The spectacle of gladiators fighting each other to the death at the Colosseum in the cause of entertainment has been replaced by reality TV and vacuous game shows, where we can watch vulnerable or simply silly people locked up in the Big Brother House and manipulated to fight each other, or cast away on a desert island and made to do unspeakable things, or attempting to become a pop star while being humiliated by celebrity-seeking judges – while we spend our hard-earned money to ring in and vote in our millions. We create multi-millionaires of the people who mock us and destroy our values in the cause of entertainment.

Great wealth, great responsibility

I don't think it matters at all whether people make great sums of money. Most often it is a reward for working incredibly hard to build up a business over a period of time, or displaying a remarkable talent. Success should be applauded in any area of life, from business to football. But once success has been achieved and rewarded, a contribution towards helping others should become the mark of our respect. Even after buying another house in the country – a Ferrari, a boat, a plane, a football club – the super-successful have more money than they can reasonably use in their own lifetimes.

We, the public, the media, friends and family, should celebrate talent, hard work and great skill but then ask of those people – what are you doing to help those less fortunate than you? Or to save the environment? Who are you backing to make the world a better place? We should scrutinize 'show-off philanthropy' and question both the reasoning behind it and what proportion of a person's or a company's financial resources are being given.

....

'. . . the day is not too far distant when the man who dies leaving millions of available wealth, which was free to him to administer during life, will pass away "unwept, unhonored, and unsung", no matter to what uses he leaves the dross which he cannot take with him. Of such as these the public verdict will then be: "The man who dies thus rich, dies disgraced."'

Andrew Carnegie

....

We almost invented philanthropy in these islands. The Victorians created huge wealth, but they also created schools, libraries, villages for their workforces, and started many of today's important social movements – like the Salvation Army and Barnardos. They were energised by their new wealth, their religion and an expanding economy, and the rich were keen to show that their new-found wealth was accompanied by a sense of morality and social conscience.

It is one of the sad facts of life that, in our Elizabethan age, the wealthiest sections of society give very little of their hard-earned cash to the poorest. People who have accumulated wealth generally keep it safely tucked away and ignore the plight of the needy. With a few honourable exceptions, like the Sainsbury family, philanthropy in Britain is much more show than substance. All this is in sharp contrast to America, where the creation of wealth comes with an accepted obligation to your local community.

It is not the bonus, or the huge annual salary, or what private bankers rather quaintly call 'a liquidity event' that accompanies the sale or public offering of a company that matters. It is what people do with the proceeds. Ditto the earning capacity of hugely talented sports stars, actors, pop idols and singers.

Be grateful for their talent to entertain and amuse, but ask them to be part of our society too. Let's have more Jamie Olivers and Joanna Lumleys, championing causes and using their celebrity to make hugely positive waves.

An Age of Generosity

It is not just the super-rich who must act. If we want to save the world, we must all move on from the Age of I into a new Age of Generosity.

We know that we've been living in a daft manner that is unsustainable. We realise that we have been foolish, that we have been 'had' by bankers and insurance salesmen, by money-lenders, advertisers and too-clever-by-half marketing folk. But we have learned our lesson. We can have another go ourselves to build a fairer, more generous world. As the visionary E. F. Schumacher wrote back in 1973 'infinite growth does not fit into a finite world.'

We need to make a real effort to learn about the issues that have an impact on our lives and our world, instead of relying on the uninformed opinions of our friends or biased commentators. We must question our politicians, business-people and church leaders. Ask them the simple questions 'Why' or 'Why not?' repeatedly until we get a satisfactory answer; demand to know what they are actually, actively doing to solve the problems that we all know we face. We should confront the lobbies that persuade our politicians to build more airports and tarmac over our countryside. We should ask the managers and heads of our supermarkets how they dare to throw good food away every day when people remain hungry in the same town, and the retailers of our clothes why they are being made by children who should be in school. And we must ensure that those who say it cannot be done do not stand in the way of those who are doing it. What governments fail to do we, as individuals, can.

Erich Fromm's classic 'To Have or To Be?, published over thirty years ago, stresses the human need to belong. 'A society whose principles are acquisition, profit and property,' he wrote, 'produces a social character orientated around having, and once the dominant pattern is established, nobody wants to be an outsider, or indeed an outcast.'

So if we wish to change the dominant pattern to one of generosity, enough of us need to act to create a tipping point where such behaviour is seen as the norm. Our future may depend, quite literally, on a conscious decision to live our lives in a more generous manner. We can embrace the technology that enables us to connect worldwide and the power it gives us as individuals to spread the word about our 'Generous Gene.' It is up to us.

2. Generosity

Real generosity toward the future lies in giving all to the present

ALBERT CAMUS

We are all generous

On January 10th 2010 a huge earthquake flattened much of the island of Haiti, and the people and countries of the world responded immediately and generously, sending in medical supplies, doctors and nurses, disaster teams, food, troops and money. As did seven-year-old boys.

Charlie Simpson raised over £200,000 for the Haiti earthquake victims. He had initially set out to raise a more modest £500 for Unicef's Haiti appeal by pedalling five times round the local park with his Dad. But as news of his efforts spread, thousands of people donated cash to his internet fundraising site.

Charlie's Mum takes up the story. "He was really upset by the pictures on TV. He actually burst into tears. He sat on my lap and we had a chat about the things he could do. He decided to do the cycle ride and he made me do a sponsorship form for him and that was it. We sent it out onto the web and it just went everywhere."

Full marks to Mum for setting up his sponsorship page on the Just Giving website. It was there that his story was picked up by TV stations. Even so, Charlie's efforts are a wonderful example of spontaneous generosity, of a little chap just getting on with it and how he inspired and touched others to support him. A seven-year-old catalyst for aid.

In the same month, and on a very different level, Britain was blanketed in deep snow and the country ground completely to a halt. Day after day stories of people helping each other out appeared in the press, on radio talk shows and TV. People who could easily have stayed tucked up in bed and phoned in sick, didn't, but drove the snowploughs, the gritting lorries, the trains and buses, the ambulances and ran the emergency rescue services. This is the real Britain and its people, a generosity of spirit that restores our faith in human nature.

Neither of these examples of spontaneous generosity (and there are thousands more) were initiated by the thought that the people involved might get something back. Young Charlie Simpson didn't watch the developing horror of Haiti on his TV and think to himself – 'If I go on a cycle ride with my Dad and raise £500 for children in Haiti, all my friends will think I am a good person.' Neither did any of the millions of people who gave to the victims of Haiti, the tsunami, the Chinese and Italian earthquakes or any other disaster. They did it because they felt a common compassion for the shocking scenes that were unfolding before their eyes, and because they wanted to do their bit to help.

And in the case of the little local problem of 'too much snow one winter', people who could help did help, from farmers with tractors rescuing drivers from snowdrifts, to people taking care of their elderly neighbors. These numerous acts of spontaneous generosity are not the stuff of 'research', or psychological studies and all that mumbo-jumbo; they are just what ordinary people do, when a humanitarian disaster strikes or the weather pattern swings left instead of right.

I just don't have the time

Human beings are naturally generous souls, capable of out-standing and remarkable acts of generosity when we sense the need. It is just that so often we are so caught up in the general hurry of our lives that the opportunities to help others, to give or simply lend an understanding ear pass us by.

It is all to easy to find an excuse. We are too busy – just get-ting through every day is enough of a struggle; pressure of work; responsibilities to our families; we hardly have enough time to see our friends. We feel overwhelmed – what on earth can we do to help when there are millions starving in Africa? Or simply sceptical – what is the point of doing our bit to save the environment when the Chinese are building new coal-fired power stations every hour?!

We don't know how to give, don't believe our money will really get through to the people who need help. We do enough already, don't have the time, can't help everyone. It all gets sto-len by corrupt governments and finally, sorry, charity begins at home – I need enough money left to look after myself and my family in our old age.

I am sure that there isn't a person reading this who doesn't recognise and sympathise with one or more of these barriers to living in a more generous way. But the truth is that gener-osity is an attitude to life, one that involves a compassionate heart, an open mind and a willingness to learn. And then action, to follow it through.

•••

'What we think, or what we know, or what we believe is in the end of little consequence; the only consequence is what we do.'

John Ruskin

•••

What is generosity?

Generosity is a positive and outward-looking attitude, a quality that we instinctively recognise as good. We all like to be considered generous and we admire generosity in others, as much as we abhor and dislike meanness. We enjoy being generous to our family and friends and when we have the opportunity it touches the better part of us, and we simply feel better about life.

This is not an intellectual issue, something we need to learn, to have proved to us or be told – it is instinctive. We are moved by acts of kindness, feel compassion for the plight of others, are inspired when we witness heroic or seemingly impossible human achievements, are stirred by soppy, emotional stories and films, by happy endings and rousing music.

Generosity comes from the same spot that will spur us to do anything for one of our children or for the person we fall helplessly in love with. That impulse is touched deeply by someone who has done something generous and thoughtful for us, or has forgiven us for a mistake we have made. It is part of the spiritual bit in us that links with compassion and love – difficult to pin down and analyse but something we know, when used, brings joy and gives us meaning. Generosity helps us stay well and keeps us sane.

THE GENEROSITY OF THE POOR

When she heard I was writing this book, my friend Olly carried out an impromptu survey for me in West Bengal (one of the poorest states of India). She asked fifty people what they immediately thought of when they heard the word 'generosity.'

The rickshaw wallahs, taxi drivers and market-stall holders all answered along the same lines: "open heartedness;" "giving time to those you love;" "caring for family and friends;" "giving your love and spirit." The western tourists in the hotel, when asked the same question, replied "giving money to charity;" "buying big presents for others." Different lives, different values and a clear divide between the personal and the material

I guess that is one of the issues. We don't research the attitudes of the rickshaw wallahs of West Bengal that often. They don't have similar lifestyles or values. Exactly. Generosity is more fundamental to their everyday lives.

When we put ourselves first, whether as individuals or as nations, and succumb to our 'selfish gene', we create inequality and suffering. When we work together towards a common goal we can achieve truly great things. The abolition of slavery, the winning of votes for women, the end of apartheid and the achievement of peace in conflicts such as Northern Ireland, all required people to act together, with generosity. Independence is fine but interdependence, pooling our talents to solve problems together, is an infinitely more constructive way to build a better world.

I believe that human beings are hard-wired to be generous. Generosity is a natural human instinct as well as a positive approach to living. It is taking an active interest in the world outside our immediate existence and in people other than ourselves.

Generosity was essential to successful societies long before 'civilization' arrived. Sharing tasks and looking out for each other was a key element of survival. The earliest hunter-gatherer societies (which existed for 85,000 years before agriculture started a mere 12,000 years ago) depended on co-operative work and collective decision making, with everyone pitching in to hunt, forage, cook and build shelters according to their skills, experience and aptitude.

There was no personal acquisition, no social or power-based hierarchy. Men and women contributed in different ways and were equally valued. Different people would take the lead depending on what needed to be done. In short a generous, sharing community.

By contrast, most of the societies we recognise today as 'developed' and 'civilised', are typified by the constant and relentless pressure to become independent and financially secure (whatever that means), and by the growth of consumerism to the point where we are encouraged to shop till we drop and judge people by visible signs of success, rather than by who they are. These pressures have eaten away at our value system and hardened our hearts. Work hard, play hard, spend all you can. 'Life's a bitch – and then you die.'

In becoming consumers we have lost the generosity that is natural to us – what we might recognise as the generosity of the poor; the generosity of our hunter-gatherer ancestors. And the more successful we become, the harder it may be to tackle that selfish gene. According to the Charities Aid Foundation, the richest twenty percent of the UK population give 0.7% of their income to charity, in contrast to people with lower incomes donating 3% on average. Wealthier folk make more noise and give larger sums in total, but a much smaller proportion of their wealth.

Fundamentally, though, generosity is not about money but about a willingness to share, unselfishly, with an open heart, an open hand and an open mind. It is a measure of your self worth, not your net worth. If you have enough of the stuff, it won't do you any harm at all to regularly give away a little of your income, or wealth, to help people less fortunate than yourself. But there's more to it than that. People who don't focus on acquiring things don't fear losing them. They are the people who value enjoyment, friendships and sharing.

....

'I believe we have a fundamental human need to give. We all need help in our own lives, we all need to give. At a funeral or memorial service you never hear people say, "He made a lot of money, he had three boats." You hear, "He was generous, sincere, always had time for people." Those are the things that we value in others and we value them in ourselves. We feel better for giving.'

David Robinson, founder of Community Links and We Are What We Do

....

How to be generous: an open heart, an open hand and an open mind

Opening our hearts gives us an opportunity to pause, a chance to think about others, to love them and to look for ways to care for them, without making judgements or expecting to receive something in return.

Encouraging people is generosity. Practise giving compliments, telling people that they have done something very well, that they can win if they keep going, that they are fab, talented, kind – so often words of encouragement from other people, at a critical moment, provide the spark we need to carry on with our hopes and plans and dreams, to move forward and not give up. Showing that you believe in someone is incredibly powerful and generous

An open hand invites us to get off our backsides and do something, to be pro-active in helping others, to come alongside when they need us.

Sharing what you have with others is generosity. First and foremost, sharing your time and contact. Someone who is housebound or ill will be counting the time in slow-motion until the next person makes them aware they're not forgotten, even if it's only by email. Practise sharing a meal (there's probably no need to buy extra – it'll go round), your expertise, your hospitality, or even a bed for the night. No cost at all.

An open mind teaches us to listen, to learn and to look at people and their problems from a different and more compassionate angle. To refrain from making judgemental or daft remarks, but to hear others' points of view. This is possibly the most important quality required to lead a generous life.

ARTI'S GRANDPA

My friend Arti's grandfather was a doctor in India who treated all who were sick, whatever their caste or religion. He was inspired by Florence Nightingale, the nineteenth-century founder of nursing who treated all wounded soldiers, irrespective of which side they were on. She argued that it was her job to treat all mankind.

During the day, he treated his patients in the hospitals, but in the evenings he treated those who couldn't afford medical help. He had a surgery built onto the family home and every evening a constant stream of people, too poor to pay for any medicine, would come to see him. He would treat them using the same professional skill and care that he did with his hospital patients. There was always a pot of tea on the go in the house, and anyone and everyone came to dinner, from the poor who needed a decent meal to respected Hindu saints and sages.

In those days, the patients, though poor, lived close to the land; many had livestock, or grew fruit and made hay. In the mornings Grandpa would often find that his sheep and goats had been washed – it being a tradition that all the animals were washed once a day. Or a bowl of fruit would be left outside his door, or some freshly cut hay delivered for his animals. The people had little, but from what little they had, they gave generously.

Grandpa's example left a mark on Arti and her brothers and sisters. In Arti's words they all learned that "being generous is just something you do because it is something you saw done. It is natural. You don't need to educate people to be generous – we are made to give, we do it naturally and because we have seen someone else do it. When we don't give we hurt ourselves."

• •

Finally, rewarding yourself is generosity. It is good to be generous to yourself sometimes, in fact hugely important. Buying yourself a treat, as pure self-indulgence or as a reward for something achieved, is good news. It warms up your Generous Gene! Of more practical use is to learn how to forgive yourself for falling short, and refusing to beat yourself up for your own perceived weaknesses; for not getting the job you really wanted; for your share of the breakdown of a relationship. Accept yourself for what you are and where you're at. Give yourself a break and move on. We all fail sometimes, but to dwell on a mistake is to remain anchored in the past.

Forgiveness

Forgiveness is generosity. Forgiveness and moving on ought to be a no-brainer, but is perhaps the toughest of all generous acts. Forgiving people for things they have said or done (or things you *think* they have said or done) that have made you angry, or perhaps hurt you, is hugely difficult and takes great courage. It can be hard to forgive yourself, perhaps for not having done all that you could in a relationship. Ultimately, though, the choice is between continuing to harbour bitterness, or embracing the positive impacts of healing.

It is difficult when the person you need to forgive has done something really unacceptable, or when they are not in forgiving mood and you have to continue making the effort and keeping the door open. But there is a simple truth about forgiveness – it is an act of choice. You can choose to forgive someone for something they have done, feel the weight lifted off your shoulders and move on. Or you can refuse forgiveness, and carry the mistrust or hatred with you to your grave. If you think it impossible, remember the example of South Africa's Truth and Reconciliation process or Northern Ireland's Peace and Reconciliation initiatives. Is your issue that big?

UBUNTU

· ·

'In our African culture, there is something very difficult to put into English – 'ubuntu'. Ubuntu speaks about the essence of being human. We say that a person is a person through other persons . . . that it is impossible to be human as a solitary individual . . . that we are created for inter-dependence, and my humanity is caught up in your humanity. I need you to be all you can be in order for me to become all I can be. Forgiveness is therefore not altruistic but is instead the best form of self-interest. Conversely, a person who dehumanises another is also dehumanised.'

Archbishop Desmond Tutu – Chair of the Truth and Reconciliation Commission

· ·

After twenty-seven years in jail, most people expected Nelson Mandela to emerge hungry for revenge. But instead of retribution he urged his own people to work for reconciliation. And, leading by example, he invited his former jailer to attend his presidential inauguration as a VIP guest.

In a cynical world, South Africa's guiding principle in its search for a non-racial and inclusive democracy was stated by Mandela thus: 'the principle that there are good men and women to be found in all groups and from all sectors of society; and that in an open and free society those South Africans will come together to jointly and cooperatively realise the common good.' Mandela's vision was for South Africa to fly the flag as 'an inspiration to many. We signal that good can be achieved amongst human beings who are prepared to trust, prepared to believe in the goodness of people.'

Learning to forgive is one of the hardest things to do, but also one of the most generous, and liberating.

Generous work

Some people work to earn money, some people's work is their life. Yes they do get paid a wage, but their work involves commitment and a large helping of generosity. They do jobs we all rely on, but they work for reasons over and above the pay they receive.

If your house caught fire this evening, a group of very skilled, brave men and women would arrive in a fire engine and put the fire out. Possibly rescuing you from an upstairs window, or saving your life. And perhaps risking their lives in the process.

If you set off one morning to drive to work and were involved in a serious crash on the motorway, the emergency services would be there quickly to administer first aid and if necessary cut you free from your vehicle and ferry you to hospital.

When you have a baby, various people in the NHS including nurses, doctors and midwives are there for you to help bring 'the most beautiful baby ever born' into the world.

Our children are taught, sometimes against all the odds, by teachers dedicated to passing on their hard-won knowledge and inspiring each child to learn, pass exams – or even just to read and write properly. Social workers – constantly attacked by the media – work unbelievable hours doing gruelling jobs that we turn our faces from.

When commentators talk about heavy case-loads, what they really mean is that one individual or a small group working in a very deprived area is experiencing dozens of instances of frightening behaviour and shocking poverty on a daily basis every day of the year.

Then there are nurses, and student nurses; hospital cleaners and porters; policemen and prison officers; railwaymen and bus drivers; advisers in job centres. These are the people who should be our real heroes, the ones who truly make a difference and contribute to our lives and communities. Sometimes I am tempted to conclude that people are paid in inverse proportion to their value to society. Local government refuse collectors and road sweepers £18,000 and £16,000 , Ambulance staff £22,000, Nurses £29,000, a private in the army in Afghanistan £20,000, primary school teachers £33,000 – the list would be never-ending. It is hardly surprising that ordinary men and women in Britain get very angry when bankers and business leaders receive huge bonuses for betting on the derivatives market, or advising on the hostile takeovers of companies, or overspending on over-running maintenance work. And are then paid off again after ruining the businesses, banks or utilities of which they were supposed to be the stewards.

SHAUN'S PHYSIOTHERAPIST

One day I visited a school in Edinburgh and was introduced to a young man called Shaun. He was blind and had cerebral palsy – so he couldn't see, or move about independently. He was asked to show me how his new powered wheelchair worked, so he set off on his own round the school – the wheelchair had a laser on the bottom that followed a track from his classroom to the dining room – and arrived back to much applause from his friends.

On the way out his physiotherapist thanked Whizz-Kidz and myself for helping to change Shaun's life. Then she said, softly, that it had taken her two years to show him how to manage the wheelchair's controls. That is generosity of a truly wonderful kind. We said goodbye, he gave me a hug and I left. And I just sat in my car alone, crying. And deeply humbled.

Intellectual generosity: beware of clever people

There seems to be some kind of unwritten law that deliberately daft and controversial views and offensive opinions get more media attention than generous views and intelligent debate. It is the art of journalism to get a decent debate going and good news, as we know, isn't news.

There are highly qualified, clever people who attack everything and everyone. They are normally on the sidelines, slinging intellectual arrows, unruffled by the battlefield. Normal people who go on to achieve remarkable things often do so despite their faults and in the face of bitter opposition from clever people; not forgetting vested interests and lobbyists. William Wilberforce, Martin Luther King, Gandhi, Nelson Mandela and many others are now heroes where once they struggled to effect change, suffered greatly for their views and were attacked continuously by those defending the status quo.

Controversy outsells a 'good news' story every time. When Mother Teresa died, a small section of the media had a field day. What she had achieved, and the love she was given by people all over the world, was tarnished by stories of accepting money from unclean sources and photographs of her holding hands with Michele Duvalier, wife of former Haitian dictator Jean-Claude Duvalier.

Author and journalist Christopher Hitchens capitalised on people's interest by producing the film *Hell's Angel: Mother Teresa of Calcutta*, an attack on her international 'sainthood'. It's all too easy to focus on the more controversial aspects of her Catholic faith and her work – her stand against artificial birth control, views on abortion and belief that women should not be priests. It was alleged that her hospitals offered sub-standard medical treatment, the way they were run was not up to scratch. Would the beggars who died peacefully, loved and cared for the by the sisters, agree with him?

Thankfully, the majority of people just shook their heads in disbelief and ignored the clever folk. Mother Teresa had done too much; touched too many lives, made too much of a difference for journalists to change our view. With God's help and large amounts of determination, hard work and commitment. Final answer.

Generosity and faith

'Do unto others as you would have them do unto you'

(GOSPEL OF MATTHEW, CHAPTER 7, VERSE 12)

Generosity is a virtue shared by all people, whether they belong to a faith, are confirmed atheists or whether – and this group will number millions throughout the world – they are 'don't know'. Generosity is admired and practised in all cultures and all faiths and is non denominational.

The Age of Reason was going to bring an end to faith. Faith only existed because we couldn't explain, or didn't know, what science was bound to explain – it was based on ignorance and superstition. The rationalists and anthropologists who predicted that human evolution would wipe out faith have been proved wrong. You may think that we live in a faithless world, where the majority don't believe in a god or higher being. But you are wrong. Christianity is keeping pace with the growth in the global population, Islam is growing faster. There are roughly 6.6 billion people in the world, and of these more than 2 billion are Christian, 1.3 billion Muslim, 800 million Hindu and 500 million Buddhist.

Total that up and around 70% of people belong to major world faiths, even before factoring in the many smaller religions and the growth in shamanism, paganism, witchcraft and spirituality in all its guises – it seems we need faith more than ever today to make sense of our world.

Everyone has a spiritual life. A significant majority believe in a higher being or beings who created the world and who answers prayers. The major world religions and faiths have endured, fundamentally shaping history.

Perhaps we need reminding that all world faiths stress the importance of helping less fortunate members of society. All place great emphasis on generosity, giving both money and love, quietly and with humility.

In Judaism, *Tzedakah* (literally 'righteousness') is more than charity. The word's root is related to justice and the obligation of *Tzedakah* rests on everyone, rich and poor alike. Moses Maimonides, the greatest Jewish thinker of the entire pre-modern period – philosopher, physician, legal and ethics scholar – devised eight levels of *Tzedakah*. The highest level enables a person to become self-sufficient by providing him/her with a job or other means of financial support. The next four champion generosity and anonymity, excluding the possibility of being rewarded by being known as generous. Thereafter, real generosity slips – the donor gives graciously and sufficiently but only after being asked; the donor gives cheerfully, but less than is appropriate; the giver gives begrudgingly and less than needed.

Maimonides' thinking on generosity can be summed up briefly. A person who gives only after being asked is not really generous; giving less than is appropriate is mean; giving begrudgingly makes you not a nice person. He taught that the method of giving charity is an integral part of charity itself

SHAKESPEARE AND COMPANY

'Be not inhospitable to strangers, lest they be angels in disguise' – sign in Shakepeare and Company, Paris.

Shakespeare & Co is one of the most famous shops in the world for 'book people'. By the side of the river Seine, looking out over Notre Dame, its owner George Whitman has been running what he calls "a socialist utopia masquerading as a bookstore" for fifty years. At Shakespeare & Co, young authors and artists can sleep in the shop free – there are thirteen beds tucked away among the wonderful selection of books, message boards and rickety staircases.

There are a few house rules – guests must agree to make their bed in the morning, help out in the shop and read a book a day. George, now in his nineties, reckons that more than forty thousand people have slept in the shop at one stage or another.

It may be eccentric behaviour, but it is also generous. A recognition that there is more to life than using sales space just for sales.

One of the most important principles of Islam is that everything belongs to Allah, and that wealth is held by human beings in trust. One of the five pillars of Islam, *Zakat*, meaning both 'purification' and 'growth', is firmly established in the Qur'an as obligatory. It is the amount of money that every mentally stable, free, and financially able Muslim, male or female, has to pay to support specific categories of people.

Setting aside a proportion of what you have purifies you. Cutting back on your needs balances and encourages new growth. For most Muslims, this involves an annual payment of 2.5 per cent of capital.

Generosity has a very strong cultural base. Many of the characteristics of Arab society are found in their strongest form in Bedouin culture. Bedouin are most famous for their hospitality or *diyafa*. One of their core values, rooted in the harshness of desert life, is never to turn a traveller away. Any stranger, even an enemy, can approach a tent and be sure of three days' board, lodging and protection after which he may leave in peace. Bedouin will always offer their guest a rich meal, even if they have to slaughter their last sheep or borrow from neighbours to do it. Their honour is bound by their hospitality and lavish generosity.

Hindu culture teaches that God could come to visit your home, and when he does he will come as a stranger to whom you must offer food and shelter. If you really want to know God, he is in the strangers – so no one should leave your house without at least a glass of water.

• •

Teach this triple truth to all: a generous heart, kind speech, and a life of service and compassion are the things which renew humanity.

Buddha

• •

The Buddhist concept of sympathetic joy arises when someone regards all human beings with loving kindness and rejoices in their good fortune. By overcoming resentment, envy and jealousy, and finding inspiration in the happiness and accomplishment of others, an individual can begin to understand how solid and genuine shared happiness is. Buddha saw *dana* – generosity of spirit, giving and receiving from the heart – as both the generous act of giving and the gift itself.

Jesus, too, was a believer in generosity. Take the story of the widow's mite, as told in Luke's gospel:

'Jesus sat down opposite the place where the offerings were put and watched the crowd putting their money into the temple treasury. Many rich people threw in large amounts. But a poor widow came and put in two very small copper coins, worth only a fraction of a penny.'

'Calling his disciples to him Jesus said, "I tell you the truth, this poor widow has put in more into the treasury than all the others. They gave out of their wealth; but she, out of her poverty, put in everything – all she had to live on".'

St Paul, largely responsible for creating the early Christian church, spread the word too: 'Whoever sows sparingly will also reap sparingly, and whoever sows generously will reap generously.'

Selfish Genes?

Most people have heard of Richard Dawkins' book *The Selfish Gene*, but far fewer know about his conclusion. Standing on Darwin's shoulders, Dawkins initially suggests that people consistently do things that are selfish and that benefit their genes because that's how 'survival of the fittest' works and has always worked. But then, fascinated by how we remain kind, how we help each other out and are willing to lay down our lives for each other, he eventually concludes that altruism, kindness et al is a triumph of our intelligence over our genes.

Our unique intelligence and values-driven behaviour gives us an opportunity to thwart our selfish programming. To quote:

'Our genes may instruct us to be selfish, but we are not necessarily compelled to obey them all of our lives. It may just be more difficult to learn altruism than it would be if we were genetically programmed to be altruistic. Among animals, man is uniquely dominated by culture, by influences learned and handed down.'

'If you wish, as I do, to build a society in which individuals cooperate generously and unselfishly towards a common good, you can expect little help from biological nature. Let us try to teach generosity and altruism, because we are born selfish ... let us understand what our own selfish genes are up to because we may then at least have a chance to upset their designs.'

What a wonderful challenge! History need not repeat itself. We can evolve further. Our own future happiness, and the future success and strength of our communities and societies, depend on us taking a conscious decision to abandon the excesses of selfish, individualistic behaviour that has driven (and is still driving) global industrialisation, urbanisation and commercialism.

If we keep on with the same plot, nothing will change. We need to include more generosity with the struggle to get on with our own lives, to make ends meet, and survive the slings and arrows of daily life. We, as individuals, need to turn the tide. Our very future as a species depends on nurturing and using our Generous Gene.

We have it in us. Let's bring our generous gene to the fore.

3. Happiness

It is one of the beautiful compensations of this life that no one can sincerely try to help another without helping himself.

RALPH WALDO EMERSON

What makes us happy?

Happiness is not linked to wealth. There is a certain level of income above which, psychiatrists, doctors and researchers all agree, happiness levels peak. And it is a surprisingly modest amount. We instinctively know that there is more to a happy, fulfilled life than money, and it turns out that one of the key elements is being able to make a contribution. A generous life is a happier life!

In March 2008, research by Dr Elizabeth Dunn and Lara Atkin of the University of British Columbia with Professor Michael Norton of Harvard Business School was published in the journal *Science* under the title 'Spending money on others promotes happiness'.

The learned professors wanted to check out whether spending money on others might be a more effective route to happiness than spending on oneself, so they asked a sample of

632 men and women to rate their general happiness, and only after they'd done this to provide details of their income and monthly spending. Regardless of income, those who spent money on others reported greater happiness than those who spent on themselves.

A smaller survey of a Boston company's employees before and after their bonus payments, of between $3,000 and $8,000, showed that those who had devoted more of their bonus to 'pro social' spending were happier than their less generous friends.

Contrast this with the results of increasing personal wealth. During the last five decades the average US citizen's buying power has more than doubled. In 1957 the US per capita after tax income (inflated to 1995 prices) was $8,200. By 2002 it was $23,000. Did this more than doubled wealth – enabling twice as many cars per person, as well as TVs, DVD players, laptops, air-conditioning, cell phones et al – also buy more happiness? In 2002, 30% of people claimed to be very happy, down from 35% in 1957.

Take money out of the equation altogether, as Time Magazine did when it polled over two thousand people in 2005, and the findings show that most people find happiness in family and relationships, and in helping others. In answer to the question 'What one thing in your life has brought you the greatest happiness?' the top four sources of happiness were all about others.

- 77% cited their relationship with their children
- 76% their friends and friendships
- 75% their contribution to the lives of others
- 73% their relationship with their spouse/partner or loved one.

Martin Seligman is one of the most respected happiness experts. In the late 1990s, when president of the American Psychological Association, he developed with others a new goal for psychology: Positive Psychology.

'I realised that my profession was half-baked. It wasn't enough for us to nullify disabling conditions and get to zero. We needed to ask, what are the enabling conditions that make people flourish? How do we get from zero to plus five?'

In his book *Authentic Happiness* Seligman lists three key components of happiness: pure pleasure; engagement – the depth of involvement with one's family and work, romance and hobbies; and meaning – using personal strengths to serve some larger end. It turns out that pleasure is the least important of these three. 'This is newsworthy because so many people build their lives around pursuing pleasure when engagement and meaning are much more important'.

Seligman is a proper guru. The research he has conducted into happiness is legend. In one case he asked his students whether they thought happiness came more from exercising kindness than from having fun. He spilt the class in two and the results were 'life changing'. The afterglow of the 'pleasurable' activity paled completely in comparison with the effect of the 'kind action'.

He then studied the altruistic behaviour of two groups, one happy and one unhappy. In his own words 'before I saw the data, I thought that unhappy people – identifying with the suffering they know so well – would be more altruistic.'

'So I was taken aback when the findings on mood and helping others without exception revealed that happy people are more likely to display more empathy and are willing to donate more money to others in need. When we are happy, we are less self-focused, we like others more and we want to share our good fortune with strangers. When we are down, though, we become distrustful, turn inward and focus defensively on our own needs.'

Random Acts of Kindness

Sonja Lyubormirsky, a respected psychologist at the University of California Riverside, found that people who take the time consciously to count their blessings every week report a significant increase in their overall satisfaction with life. Expressing gratitude and practising random acts of kindness also contribute a great deal to personal happiness.

Lyubormirsky suggests that 'these should be both random – let that harried mom go through the checkout queue before you – and systematic – take Sunday supper to an elderly neighbour. Being kind and generous to others, whether friends or strangers, triggers a cascade of positive effects. It makes you feel generous and capable, gives you a greater sense of connection and wins you smiles, approval and reciprocated kindness – all happiness boosters.'

••

Do all the good you can
By all the means you can
In all the ways you can
At all the times you can
To all the people you can
As long as you can

John Wesley
••

Saying thank you. Something that simple – preferably in person – to anyone you feel has helped you in life has been proved by Seligman to make people feel measurably happier and less depressed for a month. His tests show the impact takes three months to wear off entirely. Lyubormirsky goes one further with the principle of counting your blessings. Just by recording three things about their day that have gone well, and why, 'people are less depressed and happier six months later.' That's an uplifting result from not even being generous to others but being generous to yourself!

The Secrets of Happiness

During my research for links between happiness and altruism, I piled up the authors to skim through. When I came to Richard Schoch's 'The Secrets of Happiness', skimming was not enough. Three hours after picking up his book I was still totally engrossed. Schoch is a pleasure to read as he explores 'three thousand years of searching for the good life' – the philosophical and religious traditions of happiness over the centuries. His book is full of wonderful common sense, such as his thoughts on caring:

'We care about the integrity of our values and beliefs. We care about our accomplishments. We care about leaving a legacy to the world. We care about the well-being of the people in our lives. And, if we are being magnanimous, we care about the well-being of people not in our lives. All these cares bind us to the world – through what we believe, what we achieve and whom we love. This is the ultimately moral shape of each person's happiness and what makes it inseparable from – in truth dependent upon – the happiness of others. Happiness may and probably will begin with pleasurable feelings; but it will also go beyond them because happiness isn't really about feeling good – it's about being good. The problem is that we are apt to mistake the former for the latter.'

Schoch expands this thought later in the book;

' ... *everybody*, no matter who they are, what they are like or what they do, can find happiness in a way that is right for them ... our path to happiness must begin on our doorstep, where we live; otherwise it is not ours. We do not have to forge a new life – the one we have will do just fine – nor must we wait for a more opportune moment – the right moment is always now. To be happy we must rub *with* the grain of our character, not against it; we must become the perfected version of the person we already are, not someone who we could never be.'

To be happy we must rub with the grain of our character, great stuff!

HOW TO BE HAPPY

....

'Happiness is a function of fulfilment. When people are able to express their creativity, when they have meaning and purpose in life, when they have meaningful relationships and are able to make other people happy, in general they are happy then. Focussing beyond self – happiness increases helpfulness – those who feel good do good. But doing good also makes one feel good.'

Deepak Chopra; author, doctor and spiritualist

....

Further endorsement comes from Christopher Peterson of the University of Michigan. His research focus has been to define human strengths and virtues such as generosity. His conclusions: 'Giving makes you feel good about yourself –

when you are volunteering you are distracting yourself from your own existence and that's beneficial. More fuzzily, giving puts meaning into your life. You have a sense of purpose because you matter to someone else'.

'Being generous to another person enhances health by pushing aside negative emotions such as sadness/depression, fear/anxiety, and anger/hostility. It is difficult to be angry, resentful or fearful when one is showing unselfish love toward another person.'

What is the point of you?

None of these ideas are new. Abraham Maslow's 'Hierarchy of Needs' was first published in 1943. Maslow was a psychologist who organized human needs into three broad levels: physiological (food, water, a roof over your head); psychological (love, self esteem, safety and a sense of belonging); and self-actualisation (the ability to make the best use of your talents, personality and capabilities). Self-actualisers are always striving to develop and express themselves. Once we have met our basic needs, Maslow argued, we begin wanting to be useful, to have meaning.

What we're all searching for is a sense of purpose. We are urged not to 'give up on life.' In Viktor Frankl's remarkable and powerful book, *Man's Search for Meaning*, based on his personal observations of survival in a Nazi death camp, he concluded that man's search for meaning was the primary motivational force in his life: 'This meaning is unique and specific in that it must be fulfilled by him alone; only then does it achieve a significance which will satisfy his own *will* to meaning.'

Purpose in a death camp was linked to dignity and survival, but today we could honestly argue that purpose is about generosity. Without it we create an unequal society and one that is never at peace.

Multi-million-selling management experts such as Stephen Covey also teach that a sense of purpose is a critical component to a successful life. In his book *First Things First*, written with Roger and Rebecca Merrill, Covey updates Maslow's thinking by identifying four core needs: to live, to love, to learn and to leave a legacy. He defines them this way:

- To **live** is to take care of our physical need for food, shelter and clothing.

- To **love** is to recognise our social need to love and be loved, and to relate to others.

- To **learn** is to realise our mental need to develop and grow.

- To **leave a legacy** is to acknowledge our spiritual need to have a sense of purpose, personal consequence and contribution.

We have to perfect the first three needs simply in order to navigate our way through life, but to experience a life truly worth living, in Covey's view, we must leave a legacy.

Every one of us is unique. We all have a great opportunity to leave the world a better place than when we arrived. We are alive for such a short while, perhaps seventy years, and much of this time is spent simply learning about life and how to navigate our way through it. Working, sleeping and eating. Week by week, year by year. But we need to carve out some time to leave our own mark on the world, before our life is used up.

How will you have used the 'gift of life'? The answer will be important to you at the end of your life, so it really is worth asking the question now. The saying 'No-one ever said on their deathbed that they wish they'd spent more time at the office' is slightly glib, but true. The deal done or missed, the salary or promotion won or lost will not really matter.

But you *will* wish that you had spent more time with your family and friends, made up that quarrel, and been more generous to others with your time and money. You will hope that you have left the world a little bit better off for your presence.

LIFE IS NO BRIEF CANDLE

'This is the true joy in life. . . . Being used by a purpose recognised by yourself as a mighty one. . . . Being a force of nature instead of a feverish, selfish little clod of ailments and grievances complaining that the world will not devote itself to making you happy. I am of the opinion that my life belongs to the whole community and as long as I live it is my privilege to do for it whatever I can. I want to be thoroughly used up when I die. For the harder I work the more I live. I rejoice in life for its own sake. Life is no brief candle for me. It is a sort of splendid torch which I've got to hold up for the moment, and I want to make it burn as brightly as possible before handing it on to future generations.'

George Bernard Shaw

Success to Significance

Many people become successful in their chosen way of life, in business and industry, the arts, the media, sport, teaching, the academic world, medicine. In fact, thank goodness, in every area of life, people become very good at what they do: taxi drivers, vicars, gardeners, builders, charity workers, fishermen, farmers, retailers, journalists and writers – if I haven't mentioned your world, forgive me. People work hard, succeed at many different levels and are usually rewarded in a suitable fashion. Or paid the rate for the job, at least.

But are they, or you, **significant**? This does not mean giving it all up to help out in a local drug rehab unit. It is about living a useful life, recognising how fortunate you are, using your resources to help others, and being worthwhile. We can all think of people we know who have either had, or who continue to have, a positive influence on our lives, and those of others around them. They are the significant ones, the people who leave their thumbprint on the world.

Others miss the point of life, fail to be remotely useful to anyone, and remain in their own world, always busy and completely caught up with their own ambitions, problems and desires. If they do help people at all it's as an afterthought – a hastily scribbled cheque. But they never really seem to be happy or at peace. Alain de Botton recently gently mocked such people – 'next time you see someone driving a Ferrari don't think 'this is someone who is incredibly greedy', think of them as someone who is incredibly vulnerable and in need of love, feel sympathy rather than contempt.'

Time and time again whilst researching this book I was told stories about the generosity of the poorest people on the planet. Those who seemed to have so little, but gave freely to strangers. In sharp contrast to the meanness of many of those who are far more affluent.

Dickens knew it when he wrote A Christmas Carol. Remember Scrooge?

'Oh! But he was a tight-fisted hand at the grindstone, Scrooge! A squeezing, wrenching, grasping, scraping, clutching, covetous old sinner. Hard and sharp as a flint, from which no steel had ever struck out generous fire: secret, self contained and solitary as an oyster. The cold within him froze his old features, nipped his pointed nose, shrivelled his cheek, stiffened his gait . . . he carried his own low temperature always about with him.'

It takes three ghostly visits for Scrooge to see the error of his ways, Finally, through the ghost of Christmas Yet to Come, he hears colleagues discussing his own funeral: "'It's likely to be a cheap funeral" – says one – "for upon my life I don't know of anybody who will go to it"'.

Scrooge, not so keen on that as a legacy, sees the light and resolves to lead a more generous life. And in writing about him Dickens reflects a universal truth. The unhappy may mock, but that should not deflect those who are doing something to improve the world.

'He became as good a friend, as good a master and as good a man as the good old city knew, or any other good old city, town or borough in the good old world. Some people laughed to see the alteration in him, but he let them laugh, and little heeded them. . . . His own heart laughed and that was quite enough for him.'

Others have proved, many times over, what we already know in our hearts – that generosity and a life lived generously makes us more content and happier people ourselves.

When a small child picks a flower, smiles because it's beautiful, then hands it over, you cannot help but smile too. You only have to pause for a moment, and think about the last time you did something because you were thinking of what might please someone else and remember how you felt about it. When you ask people to recall an act of generosity that they have received recently, they can always recall one. Often it is the small acts that both surprise and touch them. It is also one of life's rather wonderful blessings that often the less other people know of your generosity, the better you feel. A small act of kindness shared between just two people is truly special.

It's the thought that counts, but the action that matters

We can never anticipate the cards we'll be dealt by life; how long we'll live, or whether a car crash or an illness will change our future. We can and do insure our houses, health and possessions. Our pets, our teeth, our future income, our pensions. But we can't insure everything: however much we might wish for long-term security, none really exists. Focussing too much on our selves and on our futures is the antithesis of a living a happy life today, and one of the barriers to leading the generous life we would rather lead.

If our guiding principle is 'survival of the fittest' it will be over the dead bodies of the weakest members of society and a greed that will destroy – is already destroying – the limited resources of this planet. This is not something to be proud of nor, we now know, an attitude that will make us happier or more content. History, philosophy and research continue to show that a generous person is a happy person – that when an individual is actively engaged in giving and helping their fellow human beings, they feel better about themselves. And it's a win-win – happier people are more comfortable in their skins, and more generous.

4. ENOUGH

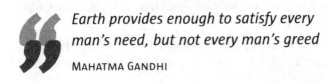

Earth provides enough to satisfy every man's need, but not every man's greed

MAHATMA GANDHI

What is enough? A paradigm shift to a more generous society

I don't think the term 'consumer society' was around much in my childhood. I was a post-war baby with parents who had learnt to live with rationing and make and mend. Come to think of it there wasn't much inflation either. But now I am a consumer in a consumer society; targeted, categorised, inundated with advertising messages and able to shop from '8 till late' seven days a week. I've been a Yuppie, a DINKY (double income, no kids yet), an Early Adopter (I like gadgets and gizmos) and am trying unsuccessfully to be an Empty Nester (despite constant encouragement to fly, my fledglings seem glued to the parental nest). We have all been shaped by consumerism and come to judge ourselves and others by what we have or buy.

We admire wealth for its own sake: 'Who wants to be a Millionaire?' is global and consumerism is expanding around the world with it. But the Age of I has brought our economy, and our society, to the brink of collapse. It is time to have a serious talk with ourselves about what is 'enough'.

We need to change the way we live. Think personally – how much do I need to live a happy, contented and fruitful life? Is the drive to own things really worth the sacrifice? As a world citizen, how am I using up the earth's ultimately finite resources?

Am I materially rich but time poor? What's that doing to my family life? How much time do I have to connect with friends? Could there be a better life out there?

It is important to do this now, as individuals and communities, because we have reached a major crossroads – financially, environmentally and spiritually. We need to set out to create a world rather than acquire it. To take only what we really need, and not more than our proper share.

The good news is that deciding what is 'enough', on a personal level, is hugely liberating. It frees us from the continuous drive to accumulate things, and saves a great deal of money by not buying stuff we don't really need, and a great deal of time then wondering where to put it and advertising the not so new stuff on eBay.

....

An investment banker was watching the sun set over the pier of a small Nicaraguan village as a fisherman docked his boat. Inside the boat were several large yellowfin tuna. The banker complimented the fisherman on his catch and asked how long it took to catch them.

'Only a little while,' replied the fisherman.

The banker asked why he didn't stay out longer and catch more fish?

'I have more than enough to feed my family and share with our friends,' said the fisherman.

'But what do you do with the rest of your time?'

'I sleep late, fish a little, play with my children, siesta with my wife, stroll into the village each evening where I sip wine and play guitar with my amigos. I have a full and busy life, señor.'

The investment banker scoffed. 'I am a Harvard MBA, and I can help you. If you spent more time fishing you could buy a bigger boat. With the proceeds from that bigger boat you could buy several boats; eventually you would have a fleet of fishing boats. You would have enough fish to sell to a processing plant with no middleman involved. You might eventually open your own cannery.

You would control the product, processing and distribution and be able to leave this small village and move to Managua. You could eventually move to New York City to run your expanding enterprise.'

'But señor, how long will this all take?'

'15-20 years,' replied the investment banker.

'But what then, señor?'

The banker laughed and said, 'That's the best part. When the time is right you would sell your company stock to the public and become very rich. You would make millions!'

'Millions, señor? Then what?'

The banker sighed. 'Then you would retire. Move to a small coastal fishing village where you could sleep late, fish a little, play with your kids, siesta with your wife, stroll into the village each evening where you could sip wine and play guitar with your amigos'.

••

Money saved either doesn't have to be earned at all, or can be used much more productively. Enough means having everything you need, but nothing in excess.

We need to go through a personal and national paradigm shift, give ourselves permission to make time for a life which is simpler and has more space in it, freeing up energy to 'sip wine and play the guitar'.

Let's take a quick look first at over-consumption of food.

Enough to Eat

According to the World Food Programme a billion people in the world are overweight, with 300 million clinically obese. At the same time the 'bottom billion' people on the planet are desperately short of food, malnourished and dying of starvation. As each year North America and Europe throw out enough food to feed the world's poor three times over, elsewhere someone dies of starvation every three seconds.

In the UK, families bin a third of all food they buy. Official studies show that an average household throws away food worth about £420 a year, while the figure for a family home is £610. So how have food manufacturers, producers and retailers managed to continually increase their sales in the UK, when the population since 1960 has grown on average about 0.5% a year?

- **Step 1**, innovate: from plain crisps, to cheese and onion, to aged gruyère and shallot.
- **Step 2**, be more visible: the more shelf space a product has in the supermarket, the more we buy. To gruyère and shallot add ten other varieties, mixed

packs, party packs, children's packs, school lunch snack-packs, multi-packs and more.

- **Step 3**, special offers: whether it's BOGOF (buy one, get one free) or two for £5, they're designed to make us buy more than we intended.
- **Step 4**, add value: pre-packed, ready washed, ready made and loaded with gunk!

We all fell for it – are still falling for it. Many of us, having tried to eat all we have been sold, are now targeted by marketing gurus selling faddy diets, herbal medicines, celebrity exercise DVDs and gyms. So when thinking about what is enough, it makes sense to start with our attitude to food consumption and waste. Why does salt have a 'sell by' date? It's a preservative. It probably came from a salt mine where it had been minding its own business for hundreds of thousands of years. Caught up in an impenetrable web of 'best before', 'sell by' and 'eat by' dates, special offers, brilliant packaging and neuro-marketing schemes (so clever you can't help but buy!), we are all enticed to buy more than we need, some of which we inevitably end up throwing away. We have become a nation of grazers and latte addicts.

John Naish observed dryly when writing about *Enough*: 'Girdled by multimillion-pound industries that use an ever growing array of overt and hidden persuaders to get us to want things, work for things and buy more of them, we don't tend to complain. But if you were physically forced by powerful gangs to spend all your time and energy in the pursuit of things you didn't need, didn't want and ultimately didn't enjoy, you'd feel sorely misused.'

We are bombarded with messages to buy more and eat more. Going round a large supermarket looking out for these messages is a very salutary experience. I know I'm being pro-grammed round, but I still find it difficult to come out with my shopping list and no more. I know the bread ('an essen-tial') will be at the furthest point from the entrance, but the nice fresh-baked smell hits my nostrils as I walk in. Mmmm, hungry already! I know the colourful fruit and veg have been put by the entrance to slow me down with a chance to handle, select and pack. I'm a sucker for that too.

There is a huge variety of foods we could and really should make at home, or that we simply don't need. How many dregs of pre-mixed salad dressings are cluttering up your cupboard? Packaged portions of peeled fresh fruit; organic pureed baby food – a small jar of 'beetroot with parsnip mash' for £1.89 (serves you right if baby throws it at you); ready-made macaroni cheese; roast potatoes ready to put in the oven; pre-cooked microwaveable rice; bottled water (WHY are we still buying water in bottles?); Skinny Water??

A rural African or Indian family would shake their heads in disbelief unless, as with powdered baby milk, marketing muscle had already convinced them it was better than nature.

Then there is 'choice'. An enormous selection of toilet paper – how strongly *do* you feel about the softness of the paper when wiping your bottom? Innovation, because '*new*' shifts product. Is the world a better place for pyramid-shaped tea bags? But that's the power of a consumer economy for you. Where the tea producer is expected to invest in the machin-ery to produce the pyramids, without any guarantee of future sales.

To add insult to injury, the content of some of this food is simply rubbish. Food manufacturers are allowed to adulterate food in a way that would have landed their medieval fore-bears in the stocks. Do you really want to know what goes into a pink sausage, a hotdog or a meat pie? Or cheap ice cream? How about a 'long life' bacon brunch, with bacon, onion and potato, in a box made in Germany – 'best before' a year and a half away. Potatoes rot. What has been done to them? What will they taste like in eighteen months? Instant cheese sauce mix has a truly sobering list of fifteen different ingredients including 'maltodextrin, dried glucose syrup, palm oil, whey powder and cheese powder (6%)' – or you could make your own with cheese, flour, milk and butter.

Tristram Stuart is the author of *Waste – Uncovering the Global Food Scandal*. If you only read one title from this book's resources section, make it Stuart's. It is as riveting as it is truly sobering. 'If affluent nations stopped throwing away so much food,' he writes, 'pressure on the world's remaining natural eco-systems and on the climate would be lifted . . . by buying more food than we are going to eat, the industrialised world devours land and resources that could otherwise be used to feed the world's poor. There are nearly a billion undernourished people in the world – but all of them could be fed with just a fraction of the food that the rich currently throw away'

Waste illustrates in extraordinary detail how much food is wasted by the six major supermarket chains from which we buy 83% of our groceries (Tesco, Asda, Morrison, Co-Op, Waitrose and Sainsbury). And some of the reasons it happens, from deliberate over-stocking because they believe customers like to see full shelves, to mistakenly over-stocking because the people making the food orders predict sales inaccurately. Acres of unwanted food are simply ploughed back into the earth – the larger than required apples, crooked carrots and excess lettuces, all of which could be sold off cheaply but are instead deliberately destroyed.

Stuart's encyclopaedic knowledge of the food industry's waste is gained first hand, not least because, as a dedicated freegan, for most of his adult life he has lived off, and had parties with, perfectly good food thrown into supermarket bins.

Start to think about the amount you waste as stacks of fivers and you might sober up. But there is another even more serious reason for attempting to get a grip. There are estimated to be a million people in the UK who don't have enough food to feed themselves and their families every week.

Enough Stuff

Over-consumption is the illness of our age. We quite clearly don't need all we buy. We chuck out somewhere between thirty and forty percent of our food, and still put on weight. We have been persuaded to change our mobile phones on average every 18 months. And yet it follows, as certainly as night follows day, that the less we spend upgrading every aspect of our lives, from our homes to our cars to our annual holidays, the more we have left to pay off mortgages, enjoy our lives and give away to others.

AFFLUENZA

As Oliver James points out in *Affluenza*, placing a high value on money, possessions, appearances (physical and social) and fame results in an obsessive, envious, keeping-up-with-the-Joneses state of mind that increases our vulnerability to emotional disorders and so becomes in part responsible for rising levels of depression, addiction, violence and anxiety. Affluenza, James believes, is the contagious disease of the middle classes. His message is 'you can choose not to do it,' and he gives us a personal example:

'There were many other changes we wanted to make to the inside of the house, having done virtually nothing to it since moving in. One day, pretty much out of the blue, the answer came to my wife: do nothing. We had a house that was easily large enough for our needs. Whilst some of it was seriously run down (grotty-looking kitchen, dreary carpets), the truth was that we were bloody lucky to have a house at all. There were all sorts of things we wanted to do, but we needed to do none of them, apart from installing a new boiler (a real need in the sense that we need hot water and heating in the winter).'

....

In the west, many of us, confronted with the simple question 'what would you like for your birthday?', find it incredibly difficult to answer. In December 2007 around a million unwanted Christmas presents were sold on eBay – many still wrapped, estimated value around £1.2 billion. An eBay spokesman said: 're-homing a present means it will find a new owner who will really appreciate it.' Isn't that thoughtful of him?! Hands up those who receive presents they really don't want, and at the same time give presents they suspect the recipient will not use/read/listen to. Join the club!

It is all a colossal waste of money, and avoidable. Think of it as a culture shift. Like cycling when you can afford to take the car. Or not buying a new outfit just because it is in the sales with a 75% discount.

Ask first, why am I buying this at all? Will it significantly enhance my quality of life? Do I really need pre-packed, ready-washed baby corn flown in from the other side of the world, new clothes for every possible occasion, twenty-nine different cook books, toastie-makers and most of the contents of a high street chemist? Do I really need – or believe in – anti-ageing, anti-wrinkle creams, instant tan, seaweed scrubs, hairsprays, false nails, bath and body milks, body butters, anti-fatigue foundation 'with vitamin EFB5 and mineral-enriched formula'. Is my sense of self and self-esteem that low? Encourage the manufacturers who found that, when they reduced the number of varieties of 'Head and Shoulders' shampoo from 26 to 15, their sales went up. It may be subliminal, but we respond well to a simpler life. This over-abundant choice and consequent spending splurge hasn't made us happier.

You might prefer to join my attractive and definitely fashion-conscious friend Susannah. She's decided to buy new clothes only when she needs them.

When she buys something new an older item from her wardrobe has to go to a charity shop, or she buys two new items and gives one away. She chooses Oxfam, who sell a huge variety of second-hand clothes under the rather lovely heading of 'Loved for Longer'! Susannah acknowledges that it is unrealistic in our culture not to spend anything on new 'stuff', but at least this has made her ask herself whether she really needs another pair of jeans. Or whether she was quite happy with the ones she had.

In a way what she is doing is simply striking out for **delayed consumption**. There is a persuasively argued case for delayed consumption in a US research report which uses the example of cars, and the sheer material cost of making them. If you replace your car every two years and your lifetime as a driver is sixty years, you'll be the proud owner of thirty cars. Keeping your car just two years longer equals fifteen fewer cars. Keep each for six years and you'll own just 10 cars – that's twenty fewer, or a third as many. And we all know that with today's technology even a six-year-old car shouldn't need much maintenance.

For an alternative delayed consumption strategy you could join Freecycle. This is a grassroots and entirely non-profit way of recycling what you don't want to someone who does. You might decide to become a member when you're moving house, have a new baby, the kids have grown out of their bikes, your exercise bike has stayed too long unused or you've decided to learn the guitar. Or are just fed up queuing at the dump. It's completely free and the stuff on offer is amazing (it pays to set up email alerts if you're a serious buyer). A quick look at one day's posts turned up (a random list) a tumble dryer, microwave, baby gates, fax machine, sat-nav, iPod, racing bike, TV and exercise mat. One person's clutter is another's must-have item. It is worth noting that charity shops no longer take electrical goods because they need to inspect and certify them before resale. As Freecycle is free, you take your own risk, but can at least get your hands on someone's unwanted fridge. Freecycle's aim is to keep things out of landfill and create, build and sustain environmentally aware communities. Since 2003 it has established 494 groups (each moderated by a local volunteer) across the UK and 4,818 worldwide. Global membership is an impressive six and a half million people, and growing.

HAVING OR BEING?

'Consuming has ambiguous qualities: It relieves anxiety, because what one has cannot be taken away; but it also requires one to consume ever more, because previous consumption soon loses its satisfactory character. Modern consumers may identify themselves by the formula: *I am = what I have and what I consume.*'

Erich Fromm, To Have or To Be, published in 1976

Enough Time

Asset rich, time poor. Never enough time. Not enough hours in the day. Time flies. These are the mantras of our age. But instead of working longer hours to earn more, borrowing more to spend more, and justifying the lifestyle because of peer pressure, we can choose to focus on what is important – our family and children, our friends and neighbours, and others living in different parts of the planet. As well as on the planet itself. We bemoan the breakdown of society but we are part of the problem, and have the power to change it.

There are thousands of UK charities working to help people in every area of our lives from children with behaviour problems or falling behind at school, to teens in gangs, the elderly, those with mental health problems or disabilities, addicts, anorexics and refugees. There are hundreds of charities working with adults who can't cope with life through stress, depression, debt or anxiety. And if you look closely enough and get rid of the jargon, a huge amount of what all of them do is simply give time: quality time, where someone listens, empathises and encourages. The buzz words are 'peer support' and 'mentoring'. One-to-one long term support, often limited to two or three hours a week, sees marked improvements in behaviour, achievement and ability to cope with life.

Thousands of people put their hands up and volunteer to 'give themselves'. Paid charity workers do it for a living. It involves having enough time to build trust, listening rather than imposing your views, empathising and encouraging rather than criticising. It works in a huge range of different situations. A couple of true stories:

An eleven-year-old being disruptive in class was about to be excluded. Given time to talk things through with a charity worker trained to listen, it turned out he was having problems reading and was so ashamed he'd resorted to doing a whole load of stuff (like climbing out of the window) to make sure no one found out. What he needed was a bit of extra support until he was sixteen and could leave school, not a spell in the 'kids we've given up on' slot! At the other extreme a senior surgeon allocated his time between NHS and private patients. Without exception his private patients recovered from surgery faster, and he was pretty sure he'd discovered why. NHS patients were allocated a ten minute pre-op discussion with him, while for his private patients he allocated thirty to forty minutes. 'Most people worry before an operation, but with a little more time they understand what's going to happen in more detail and are more relaxed about it.' It was his final year before retiring, so he took a decision. 'Sod the targets. I'm going to give every patient more time.' Recovery speed improved dramatically.

Belief that our self-worth depends on the pursuit of material wealth has left many of us in debt, hurting and in shock. Not buying things to impress in the way that we have been doing enables us to free up our enormous energies and talents to create a better and more considerate lifestyle for everyone, as well using less of the world's resources. How much more enjoyable and productive time would you have if you reduced the time spent shopping? Or working every hour God gives to earn the money to do so? Enough time to become more generous and engaged with the important issues that challenge us today? Changing the quality of your life, and the way you think and perceive things, will make a difference to you, and an even bigger difference to other people.

A PORTFOLIO LIFE
••

Charles Handy is one of the world's most influential management gurus and writers, one of the first people to develop the concept of living a portfolio life, which he explains in his book *The Elephant and the Flea*. I first met him and his wife Elizabeth on January 1st 2004 – New Year's Day. Charles had suggested they call by on their way from London to Norfolk. The fact that they had taken the trouble to see me on New Year's Day is a clue to their lifestyle.

I was a bit in awe and had gone out of my way on New Year's Eve to ensure a clear head the following morning! Charles is a gentle, friendly and quiet man who simply radiates wisdom. Elizabeth acts as gatekeeper to the Handy household. *The Elephant and the Flea* had intrigued me with its explanation of portfolio behaviour; a lifetime career replaced with a portfolio of work. In Charles' words, 'a few years ago we decided we didn't need to maximise our income; we wanted to maximise our life.'

At the start of each year Charles and Elizabeth work out how much money they need for the year ahead. Charles adds twenty percent because 'he worries', and then they plan how much they need to work to earn it. Elizabeth is a professional photographer. Charles could circle the world giving speeches and talks and be well paid for it. But he would rather live a life that he enjoys than pursue wealth for wealth's sake. In most years the Handys spend a third of the year working and earning money, a third 'studying' or writing and learning, and a third doing pro-bono work – helping people for nothing, giving speeches and so on. He and Elizabeth schedule in ninety days for leisure. He pointed out that a weekend off isn't important if you plan your life differently. And that in the right circumstances he's quite open to barter instead of payment. This began when he was asked to speak in Calcutta (en route to a paid appointment in Australia) for a very low fee. He suggested he'd be happy to waive the payment on one condition. Could his sponsor arrange introductions and a little time in his schedule to meet three of the most interesting people in Calcutta – his sponsor's choice? The people he was introduced to included Mother Teresa, and with that it became an established habit!

●●

I admit to a certain amount of jealousy that the Handys (see opposite) have got their lives so sorted! What is the point of earning a higher taxable income when you can nourish your mind and soul by meeting some of the world's most interesting people instead? In my own small way I now try to emulate the plan Charles and Elizabeth created. I split my working life into three. Part is fee-paying, advising companies and individuals about how to give to charities effectively. Part is dedicated to writing and learning more about different charities and philanthropy, which hugely informs my ability to advise clients and is fascinating and often humbling. Then an equal amount of time is spent helping out for free – supporting people managing small charities, or helping in my local church and community. Not least being around my kids more often. Nothing particularly grand or important but, all things considered, a much more balanced life.

You are probably thinking, 'it's all very well for him . . .', but the important point is that when you work out what is enough for you and do something about it, you'll be positively surprised by the improvements in your quality of life. Not everyone can rearrange their lives so radically, but many of us can try to get home earlier; plenty of enlightened employers will actively encourage charity work, some even seconding employees to work with charities; or maybe you could work four days a week – your boss may be surprisingly receptive when he realises you'll probably do ninety percent of the work you used to do, for eighty percent of the salary!

Enough to live on

I am often asked to define 'enough', and of course it is an impossible question: each unto their own. For a monk – a quiet place to live and to pray, simple food and some daily work; for an African villager – food, clean water, shelter and access to education and healthcare; for a middle-class UK parent – food, a home with enough income to pay off the mortgage, funds to support their children and a pension to sustain a reasonably enjoyable retirement. Almost exactly the same needs but hugely different costs. And if, like all of us, you're a fully paid up member of the consumer society, you probably need actively to focus on less if you're not to be carried away on the tide of more being better.

How much money do you need to live to live a happy, fruitful and purposeful life? Only you can decide. But answering this question will mark a turning point in your life, a small but important step in growing up and becoming useful and more generous.

More is better just isn't better anymore. Deep down we know it is a treadmill that we need to get off – and we can choose to do so. In our materialistic society the more we earn, the more we spend, and the more we wish to earn, in a never-ending spiral, totally disconnected from any concept of enough.

So, how much money do you need to live a happy and contented life? Really need. This is not necessarily the same as what you have programmed yourself to believe you must have.

The answer is less than you think: a roof over your head, enough food (which is not nearly as much as most of us eat), friends to support you and make you laugh, companionship, a purpose in life and very little else, though, for me, faith helps.

I can't fault the logic of the reply I got from a Yorkshire businessman when asked why he didn't expand his successful and profitable business. 'You can only sleep in one bed each night, eat three meals a day at the most and drive one car at a time.' Beyond a certain level, acquiring more things has very little practical impact on the way we live.

TITHING – 'GENEROSITY WITHOUT NOISE'

Tithing is the principle of giving a percentage of your income away to charity or good causes. It was common in many ancient societies and cultures throughout the Middle East. It is mentioned several times in the Bible. It is a tenet of Jewish law. When I first heard about tithing I felt it was out of order. Didn't people know that I had commitments – a mortgage; credit card debts; holidays to pay for; children's clothes to buy; school fees to survive; pension contributions to make for my old age? When I am financially stable, then I will gladly give money away to others. Till then, please leave me alone.

Then one day I met someone who had lost his job and still gave away a percentage of what little he had to live off. I thought, if he can do it there is very little excuse for me not to, so I started very modestly, giving just two and a half percent of my monthly income. Shortly afterwards I received a pay rise and, really as a sense of gratitude, it seemed quite reasonable to give a small percentage of that away as well. I began gradually to increase my monthly giving until it reached ten percent of my earnings. Which now includes ten percent of the profits of this book. This personal decision to live off less than you earn is important and will make you feel much better about yourself, especially when life is getting you down.

When a portion of your income and wealth is set aside for helping others you won't take yourself so seriously. Putting something back into life that creates value for others as well as yourself also helps you to be thankful for what you've got, at the same time as recognising that you can quite adequately live off less. Being able mentally to draw the line at what is 'enough' is a big step in growing up, a paradigm shift. Some people argue that the principle of tithing is flawed. A person earning £100,000 who gives away or tithes ten percent of his or her income is giving £10,000 but still has £90,000 left, which is still a great deal of money to live off, save, invest, or spend.

A person earning £10,000 a year and tithing ten percent is left with £9,000, which could and probably will make his life harder. And once someone has mentally grasped the value of tithing ten percent of their income, there is a strong chance that they will hit a mental 'giving ceiling', sit back and feel pleased with themselves that they have done their bit. But those on high incomes can easily manage ten percent and be free to give more when need be.

If you decide to tithe, should the amount be from your gross income or your net income? This has been debated for years, but I'm afraid I rather take the view that I give away a percentage of what I actually receive, i.e. my net income. Maybe I will go gross as I mature.

Enough versus Greed

Where does necessity end and excess begin? The real enemy of enough is greed. The best definition I could find for greed was 'an excessive desire to acquire or possess more than one needs or deserves, especially with respect to material wealth'. Greed is not good, nor right, as the fictional character Gordon Gekko famously declared in the film Wall Street. It is ghastly. And it doesn't work – witness the recent melt-down in the world's financial centres resulting in the bail-out of banks and mortgage companies. Lehman Bros had been around since 1850. I wonder at what stage they decided they should 'go for broke'?

In the boom years all seemed well and good and right. But long-established and respected financial giants like Lehman Bros fell because their senior managements had lost track of their liabilities, lost control of their activities, lost sight, in short, of reality. The chain of profiteers underwriting sub-prime mortgages didn't spent time focusing on where the money was coming from, or how people might be affected by their actions. They were too busy just looking after themselves. And they had no idea of what was enough.

....

'(Greed) is a sin directly against one's neighbour, since one man cannot over-abound in external riches without another man lacking them . . . it is a sin against God, just as all mortal sins, inasmuch as man condemns things eternal for the sake of temporal things.'

Thomas Aquinas, theologian and philosopher, writing in the thirteenth century
....

I am not arguing that ambition or making money is wrong. If you succeed in making a fortune, well done. Money simply needs to be used productively. It is what you do with your excess wealth that matters. Use it wisely, focus on being significant or leaving a legacy. It is only by hoarding more than you need, or spending excessively on your self-interests, that you turn success to greedy obscenity.

By the time the self-made Scottish born philanthropist, Andrew Carnegie, died in 1919, he had given away around US$350 million. Perhaps best known for his saying that 'a man who dies thus rich, dies disgraced,' his philosophy had always been to share. Carnegie believed wealth was created for the common man's greater happiness and welfare, and his staff shared in his success as partners in his companies. The Americans, without the UK's feudal history of land-owning families, are still much better at giving and philanthropy than us. In the USA those who do well are expected to give generously to their local community, church, university or arts organisation. US charity patrons and trustees accept the honour and with it clearly defined requirements for annual financial support. Unless there has been a radical change recently, in the UK, and indeed in the rest of Europe, the wealthiest section of society is by far and away the meanest. A report in 2002 claimed that the richest twenty percent of the population devote 0.7% of their household expenditure to charities while the poorest ten percent hand over 3%; proportionally more than four times as much.

There are notable exceptions, only most tend to keep quiet about it. For example, one extraordinarily successful British businessman I know has worked out how much it costs him to live each year, and he gives all of his remaining income and bonuses away. An American entrepreneur worked out when he was young how much money he needed to earn to live a comfortable life, then devised a plan to earn it and give everything else away. Which is exactly what he does. The sums he distributes quietly as a major charitable donor and venture philanthropist exceed what he lives on many times over. He makes more than most of us would dream of earning in order to give most of it away, because he has already decided in his own mind and heart what is enough. One happy man.

It is quite possible to follow that principle and help create a tipping point, a shift in attitudes, where everyone who is fortunate enough to have enough is judged by their family, friends and others by how much they have done to help their fellow man. With a tad of self discipline we would buy a whole lot less, while for those who feel they don't have enough money to be financially generous, there's no excuse not to be more generous with time.

Time to ponder, perhaps, on the values and principles we are instilling in our children and our grandchildren. One of the saddest stories ever told to me was from a major UK children's charity working with child sex workers. Why did the children do it? For one, it was the only way to get enough to buy the latest designer trainers. How do children value themselves in this logic? And if they don't value themselves, how can they possibly value others? We must divert them from the peer pressure that encourages consumerism and teach them to honour sufficiency.

The concept of enough needs to be placed back where it belongs: as a core value. Consumerism, where status is linked to being seen in designer brands and with the latest, biggest, sexiest gadgets is a non value-based life. It is possible, with a little thought and perhaps a dash of reason and humility, for all of us to work out our own take on 'enough'. And when you do this you find you are somehow magically freed and more centred. You will hugely simplify your life and liberate masses of excess energy to show an interest in the world.

Now, to get this straight, I don't believe Canary Wharf should suddenly operate a 9–5 working day. Nor should doctors and nurses. I am not advocating a life without treats, or one where you keep the lights switched off and retire to bed as the only warm place in the house. I'm with Susannah. It is by each of us being aware and doing something positive – however small or radical to our lifestyles – that change will happen. Living with sharing rather than hoarding in mind.

HOW MUCH LAND DOES A MAN NEED?

In 1886, the Russian novelist Tolstoy published a short story about greed and ambition called 'How Much Land Does a Man Need?' The story goes like this:

A couple, living in town, debate the merits of town and country living with their brother-in-law, Pakhom, a small farmer living a life of honest simplicity in the country. The conversation unsettles Pakhom, who begins to think his life would be easier if he owned more land. As luck would have it, he discovers a way to get it.

A merchant passing through his village has just returned from the land of the Bashkirs, where he has bought 13,000 acres of land for 1,000 roubles. 'There is so much land that you couldn't walk round it in a year,' he tells Pakhom. 'It all belongs to the Bashkirs, the people there are as stupid as sheep, and you can get land off them for practically nothing.'

Pakhom sets off to find this magical kingdom and discovers the Bashkirs leading a very simple and happy life. He is warmly welcomed and tells them what he has heard.

Yes, there is plenty of land, their elder agrees, and Pakhom can have as much as he likes, 'At what price' asks Pakhom? The elder replies: 'The price is a thousand roubles a day. However much you can walk round in one day, will be yours. But there is one condition: if you don't return on the same day to the spot where you started, your money is lost.'

The following morning at sunrise Pakhom puts his 1,000 roubles into the elder's hat and sets off with a spade to mark his boundaries. After several hours he starts to tire, but keeps going. 'An hour to suffer, a lifetime to live' he thinks, and takes a detour to include a particularly good hollow where flax would grow well. Then, as he heads back to his starting point and the villagers, he sees the sun begin to sink. Exhausted, he realises he has gone too far and starts to worry he will be late.

He throws off his coat, boots, flask and cap and runs towards the hill that he set off from, his heart beating like a hammer, his mouth parched and his lungs burning, and reaches it just as the sun sets. The elder is waiting, laughing. 'Ah! Fine fellow,' the elder says. 'You have gained much land!'

And with that, Pakhom's legs give way and he falls to the ground, dying of exhaustion.

Pakhom's servant digs his grave. Six feet, from his head to his heels, was all that he needed.

....

A practical suggestion: Lifestyle Offsetting

Carbon offsetting (see p.186) is one way we're being encouraged to compensate for the emissions we produce. What we can do for carbon we can also do for excess consumerism. So let's introduce 'Lifestyle Offsetting' as a way of compensating for over-the-top consumer spending. When you buy something for pure indulgence, something you want but definitely don't need, offset it with a personal contribution which either builds the social capital of your local community (time spent visiting your elderly neighbour and offering to do her shopping or cooking a meal) or helping someone living on a dollar a day elsewhere. You won't necessarily stop buying new clothes, going to the theatre or eating out when you can't be bothered to cook – but you could start by recognizing that you are lucky enough to be able to do this while millions of people in the world are starving to death.

I am as guilty. I enjoy an evening out with friends and drink wine with my meals and I've no intention of giving up (even though I'm sure my doctor would encourage it). Life's pleasures are important! But if I tot up the amount I spend on booze and offset it in some way by contributing to an African water project, or the salary of a teacher in India, I offset my indulgences. It might mean less money spent at the off-licence next month, but that would be better for me anyway.

A DINNER TO REMEMBER – AND OFFSET

This year I went to Paris for the weekend with my wife. We were planning a party there to celebrate thirty years of happily married life.

A friend suggested we meet for dinner with a colleague of hers and after a terrifying drive through the city we arrived at a small but well known fish restaurant in Montparnasse. The fish was good, the wine better and at the end a bottle of brandy was placed on the table. I can take or leave brandy but this was simply delicious. All in all a convivial and jolly few hours. The bill came to €300 for four people.

As my wife and I walked back to our hotel afterwards, slightly stunned, we reflected that the total bill would have paid the salary of a teacher in an orphanage in Southern India that we both knew well, for a whole year. Or fed an entire village in Africa. Definitely, one to offset.

....

Money spent on 'another frock' could become a micro-loan to help a group of women in Peru start a weaving business that will provide them with an income for life. Another pair of shoes could be left in the shop, and the money used to pay for the education of a child for a whole year in Uganda. Small, conscious decisions, where I put the money I would have spent aside to create a life for others. Switch my focus to a life saved and a future created. There is huge power in play when we become conscious of 'enough'. The more we realise how much we have and how little we actually need, the more generous we can be to each other.

It is tremendously difficult to change a habit, particularly one that is linked to our values and reinforced by social pressure from our nearest and dearest. We need to be secure in our motivations and goals and take a stand and we need to do it together. The seeds of change are already with us. We already fit low-energy light bulbs, turn down the heating, buy hybrid cars, get on our bikes. Saving energy, recycling stuff and buying from charity shops doesn't mean you're broke. You're simply getting off the treadmill of 'more is better' and 'new is best' – and helping the environment at the same time.

And that could be the thought that opens the door and allows the new, generous, thoughtful you to leap into action, to help others and to give. To misquote Gandhi once more 'you must be the change you wish to see in *your* world.'

Take the first step

Work out what is enough. How much do you really need to live a happy and fruitful life? Do a budget, add 20%, pause and ponder. The less you need, the less you have to work.

Offset your lifestyle. Next time you buy new clothes you want, but don't need, contribute a similar sum to a homeless charity. If you spend too much money on a meal out because you cannot be bothered to cook, give money to a hunger project. Or if you drink too much, make a donation to a water aid programme. It may not help with the hangover, but you will feel better in other ways.

Stop wasting food. Read *Waste – Uncovering the Global Food Scandal*, by Tristram Stuart: your life will never be the same again. Use food up rather than throw it out; eat your leftovers; take a shopping list to the supermarket – the thinking process alone will save you a fortune.

Before you buy any more bottled water see **www.storyofstuff.com/bottledwater/**.

Ask your local food stores how much food they throw away every day, and why?

Maximise your life, not your income. Cut down the amount of time you spend at work and get a life. No one ever said on their deathbed – 'I wish I had spent more time at the office'.

Make your own macaroni cheese, don't buy it! Roast real potatoes, boil rice, make fresh baby food – as Barack Obama said 'Yes you can'.

Buy presents that people actually want. And keep a
present list of things you would like, so that when you
are asked you can give a genuine answer. Just think of
the rubbish you have been given in the past by well-
meaning friends and family. And the well-meaning
horrors you have given them.

Do you really need a new phone/laptop/car? What would
the new one do that the current one doesn't? Keeping
the old one for an extra year could make a big difference.

Tithe. Make a decision to give away a small part of your
earnings each month to a good cause, local or global.
Start at 2.5 percent. Could you really not live off 97.5%
of your current income? And thinking through who to
give it to, and giving it, will open up whole new areas of
interest in life.

5. Poverty in Britain

If you go down to the woods today, you're sure of a big surprise

CHICHESTER – 'A CITY OF ART AND SOUL'

'There are no poor people in Britain'

Chichester is a chocolate-box city, an architectural jewel on the edge of the South Downs. A short drive north is Goodwood's famous racecourse, to the south lies Chichester harbour and marina, full of yachts, speedboats and all manner of other floating fun. The city is dominated by a beautiful nine-hundred-year-old cathedral, which has an unusual reputation for contemporary art, is home to an excellent theatre and has all the shops and eating places you could possibly want. If you've not visited, do. It is worth it. It is a wealthy place in a wealthy area, a perfect picture of traditional England at its best. Not much sign of poverty of course, no beggars on street corners; that's not the sort of image to project to tourists.

In the woods and beside the canal just outside the city,

invisible and unknown to the majority of local residents, are three tented camps of homeless people. Anyone passing by, especially during summer months, might imagine they're looking at a holiday camp site.

But they are not. Within walking distance of the city centre, seventy to one hundred people are living in the woods and by the canal, homeless and hungry, with little money and little hope. The different camps provide shelter for different groups; one for young UK residents, another for the fruit pickers from eastern Europe.

The city authorities are well aware of them and take care to ban them from the city centre. But they are unknown to the vast majority of the city's population – I have recounted the story of my visit to the camps to several astonished friends who live nearby or know the area well, and who knew nothing of the homeless.

Michael Johnson is not anyone's idea of a charity CEO. In his mid forties, small, energetic, with a streetwise vocabulary, he has spent much of his adult life in prison, including a twelve-year stretch for armed robbery 'amongst other things'. He has first-hand knowledge of the drug market as a user and a dealer and when I first meet him jokes that his current circumstances – completely broke and often hungry – are a sharp contrast to his previous brilliant career: 'I used to be a successful crack dealer once'. It was when he went to work in a homeless shelter in Bognor Regis that he discovered people living in the woods outside Chichester, and decided to help them find food and somewhere safer to live.

He's not the easiest of men to track down, but after several calls and texts Michael agrees to take me with him to learn about the Chichester homeless and to visit the camps.

Our first stop is a pub on the edge of the city. Michael has managed to persuade the landlady, whom he describes as a saint, to let three rooms to homeless individuals for £90 a week. £75 comes from social services, the guests can then either pay the £15 extra in cash or do jobs round the pub. I am introduced to a quiet young woman who talks openly about her experience of homelessness and depression.

She is fearful of going out without a close friend, and has a history of mental health problems and broken relationships. She describes her fear of living on the streets. The one homeless hostel in Chichester has ten beds for men and two for women. If more people turn up each night than there are beds for, cards are drawn – the ones who draw picture cards get a bed, the rest have to leave and sleep rough. They have a breathalyser on the door.

It is difficult to believe such a system could operate in a civilised country in the twenty-first century, but a call to the hostel confirms this is a regular process, especially in the summer. When we leave I spontaneously give the woman a hug, only be told by Michael that she rarely allows anyone to do so.

A sensible man in his forties recalls how he owned his own business making pine furniture, with a turnover of over two million pounds. The business ran into trouble and was forced to close, then his marriage fell apart and he walked out of the house with no money, soon landing in court and in prison. Now, once his divorce is settled, he is determined to rebuild his life.

We pull into a private road, near the university. Pausing to remove a black bin-liner filled with bread and sausages from the back of the car, we set off in single file through the woods until after five minutes or so I hear the barking of an aggressive dog. Michael shouts out to put him on a lead, 'I've got a visitor.' We climb over the remains of a tumbled-down wall into a clearing. One man is cooking sausages and bacon on a fire, in what looks like an upturned dustbin lid; a second is perched next to him with a can of lager. He's just arrived from Warrington where he had had a row with his friends.

A young girl looks out from one of the tents. Michael tells her he's been given a load of girls' clothes and promises to bring them round next trip. The girl is thrilled. We leave the camp, climbing back over the broken wall – say goodbye to the dog (who in fairness to dogs has been incredibly well behaved) and walk back to the car.

I ask how they would normally get food. 'They steal it,' Michael says in a matter of fact way. 'A pint of milk of the doorstep is breakfast, a packet of cheddar from a shop is lunch.' And there are some meals during the week supplied in local church halls.

What about the girl? 'Such a shame' Michael says, 'I could get her into a warm, clean place tonight, and get her food and money, but she can't leave him 'cos he beats her. If she tried to leave, she'd have to get past the dog.'

On our final stop, we pull over to a lay-by on the Chichester by-pass. Another walk, this time around ten minutes, carry-ing another bag of rolls and sausages to another camp. This time the few tents are all empty; the residents are out. A pile of bikes (one or two suspiciously new) and a large pile of cans and rubbish fill the clearing, which plainly has a rat problem. You'd never see it from the roads and the farmer turns a blind eye. This is the English camp.

After several surreal hours we are back in a church hall, drinking tea and talking about constructive ways to help. It is about 8pm when there is a knock on the door and a very friendly, respectable, middle-aged woman enters, followed by several others holding small notebooks. Time for their weekly choir practice, singing acapella. When they ask if I am local, I reply that I have just come down from London to visit the homeless people living in tents in the woods.

The local ladies look at me questioningly so I ask Michael to tell them about his work and off he goes. They are amazed and interested. Slightly hesitantly I ask the women if they are preparing for a concert and suggest that perhaps they could fundraise for the Michael's homeless project – an idea which they receive enthusiastically. They even ask Michael and his friend if they would like to join their singing group, 'we have a shortage of men' – an invitation given with the genuine friendliness and innocence of English middle-class women who have no idea they have just asked two career criminals to join their happy group.

Then I get into my car, turn the heating on, set the sat nav and drive back to London, going over and over again in my head the images of the afternoon. In less than a couple of hours I'm home with a plate of food and a glass of wine, while in the woods surrounding Chichester, unknown to the residents, one hundred people bed down for the night.

Next morning I ping off a professional and dispassionately written email to support a grant from The Body Shop Foundation for Michael's work. It is approved four weeks later.

Everyone to whom I have told this story has the same two reactions. Astonishment and disbelief. How can this be happening in the twenty-first century? It doesn't really matter whether we are the fifth, seventh or tenth richest nation in the world. All it takes is for us to get to know people as people, not as 'the homeless' or 'the scavengers'; to understand and reach out a hand of friendship, a gesture often worth a hundred times more than a shed-load of money.

We all need to get out more

We exist in circles of 'people like us'. If you've had a decent education and not ended up on benefits you may feel broke, but you can hold your head up and live in the UK with a roof over your head and enough food to keep body and soul together. We have the welfare state, the NHS, income support, state pensions, social services. So, surely, there's no real poverty in Britain?

'Not real poverty,' people insist, 'not like the terrible poverty in Africa where people face starvation and possible death on a daily basis'. Those people represent 'real' poverty and are worthy of our attention because it is not their fault: globalisation, imperialism, the impact of climate change and corruption are to blame. Conversely, the poor in Britain are somehow seen as different – undeserving – and so are viewed far less charitably. After all 'it is their fault for being so lazy', 'they shouldn't spend all their money on fags and lottery tickets' and 'if they are that poor why do they all have Sky TV?' Think of poverty in the UK and many people think of dysfunctional families on benefits or those who are irresponsible with their money. Being poor is seen as being *their* fault.

Trouble is, this doesn't correspond with reality. We believe it because we select the news we read and see only what the editors choose to put into print or broadcast. And in conversation there's never quite enough time to convince someone before they argue themselves back into the security of their comfort zone.

It was all supposed to be so different. The booming economy in the 1990s and early years of this century, which we now know was a mixture of a mirage and a casino, was meant to be a 'rising tide which lifted all boats' whereby the wealth created by those at the very top 'trickled' down to everyone else and made them better off too. In the end it has not improved poor people's lives one jot and has merely resulted in record levels of inequality.

One of the insights that comes from working in the charity sector is that some of the people who need convincing are the civil servants influencing government policy. They all mean well, but they live in a bureaucratic world that requires 'evidence', 'consultation' and 'case histories'. Decisions cannot be made lightly, for the media will tear them apart (so what's new? they'll likely tear them apart anyway). 'We need to know what works', 'We need to know how to get through to hard-to-reach minorities.' 'Well,' charities reply, 'listen to the people who are doing it.' Often understanding dawns only when a civil servant is dragged out of her office and finds herself talking to a child at primary school who's never eaten a piece of fresh fruit in her life (think food deserts, transport costs, low income and no fridge at home). And even then: 'we need to get public opinion on our side.' But the public don't know, most charities don't have enough resources to tell them and most of the media aren't interested.

It is our lack of knowledge of and sheer callousness towards people whose lives are such a struggle that has always angered me. This is not generous: it is intolerant, arrogant and selfish. But then, there but for the grace of God might I have gone had I not had the fortune to create a charity for disabled children – and gain an insight into their utterly heroic lives and the wonderful unquantifiable love of their families. I guess what I'm trying to say is that it's within *everyone's* power to create a better quality of life in Britain, because it's as much about reaching out with a generous and less judgemental attitude as it is about money. You just need to get out of your comfort zone from time to time and discover what's really going on.

The Inconvenient Truth – a quarter of this 'civilised' country is poor . . .

According to the government, 13.5 million people in the UK live in poverty, about 22% of the population. The most often used measurement of poverty is a household income that's less than sixty percent the average (median) income after housing costs. In cash terms this means from around £115 per week for a single person (less than £6000 a year) to £279 per week (around £14,500 annually) for a couple with two children under fourteen years old. Still to pay is gas or electricity to cook with and heat the room; food, clothes and all the other stuff that constitutes a basic standard of living. To say nothing of transport costs and the odd emergency. If you really think that's not poverty, try it for a while.

Poverty is a root cause of the rise in violence, drugs and gang culture as a way out of a life that doesn't seem worth living. Poverty has associated exported costs borne by society as a whole. The mental and physical manifestations of poverty cost the NHS billions each year, whilst the lost potential of poor children represents lost economic possibilities for the UK economy. In sum the existence of poverty costs us all, financially, socially and economically.

Translated into English, poverty means families and individuals not having enough to eat or to heat their homes, not having adequate warm clothing, nor any money to cope with the oven suddenly blowing up or a window getting broken. And we are not even going to discuss holidays, nights out or birthday presents. These people have simply been left behind.

In one sense the naysayers are right. The poverty people experience in this country isn't anything like the desperate poverty that is experienced by the bottom billion. It is still, nevertheless, real poverty and it is deeply shocking that in a supposedly civilised and wealthy Western country, among the richest in the world, a quarter of the population struggle to find proper housing, essential clothing and regular meals, and are constantly having to juggle bills and debt.

CALL YOURSELF POOR?

I was touched, recently, by a conversation with a Zimbabwean refugee and friend, now living in London. 'When I was living in Zimbabwe,' she said, 'we never thought of ourselves as poor. We were all in the same boat, families and friends together, getting on with life. In London, it is different. Here I am poor. I need money for the bus, money to visit friends. My family in Zimbabwe don't understand. They think I have a place to live, I have clothes, I have food. How can I say I feel poor? But I am.'

. . . and cold . . .

Age UK estimates that there are two-and-a half million older households in fuel poverty. This means (despite Winter Fuel Payments) that when you turn the heating up you don't eat – or vice versa. Age UK also reckon that one in five older people skip meals to save money for heating. The basic state pension is currently £97.65 so it's easy to spend as much as a third of your weekly income just trying to stay warm in winter.

In October 2009 the Citizens Advice Bureau reported a steep increase in fuel poverty amongst their clients. Examples include a husband, wife and thirteen year old child paying £30 a week in electricity; around 16-20% of the family income. A single lady, living alone, working full time, takes home £800 a month and pays £130 a month for heat and light – 16% of her income. In 2008 Energy Watch reported that the average annual energy bill was over £1000. Since then it has only gone up.

. . . and hungry

It may be hard to get your head round people actually being hungry in a country with cafés, McDonald's, Indian restaurants and kebab joints at every corner, but the cold truth is that many are, and that many of those are children. Pop into any inner-city state school or just talk to the teachers to find out. Time was all the kids in primary schools got free milk, now you need to qualify and apply.

Did you know there are food banks in this country? The Trussell Trust is a Christian charity running fifty-six food banks throughout Britain from a depot on the outskirts of Salisbury. It has plans to grow because it has identified need in *every town* in the UK. You possibly need to pause and think about the implications of this for a moment. Demand for food from people who can't afford it is a 'growth' market. Trussell provides food boxes designed to provide three days of nutritionally balanced food to people experiencing emotional or financial crisis. A family or individual has to be provided with a voucher by a care professional, social worker or doctor. We wouldn't want to create dependency, would we? Fareshare (a spin off from the charity Crisis) works with the food industry to redistribute surplus food and stop it going to landfill. It has twelve distribution centres so far and is planning another eighteen. They are aiming for 100,000 people to be fed – every day.

Every single day of the year, in towns and cities throughout the Britain, supermarkets throw out enormous quantities of food, while people in those same communities work hard to feed people who either have no food, or not enough. You might want to ask anyone who works in the food manufacturing and processing business or the manager of your local supermarket how they feel about this? Having demanded the perfect apple and the straight carrot we've ended up with produce at prices that a whole load of people can't afford, so it takes charities to step in and make sure the most vulnerable citizens of this wealthy nation don't become ill from malnutrition. And if you want an example of how our society and the businesses supported by us truly behave, check out Tristram Stuart's seminal book on supermarket waste.

How to work flat out and still be broke

Dr Vincent Pattison is one of the country's leading experts on UK poverty and works at the Ingeus Centre for Policy and Research. He has identified working poverty as the 'hidden' poverty in the UK – in other words even if you have a full time job you can still end up poor. This what Dr Pattison says:

'These households are not the usual suspects in the public's perceptions of 'the poor' and cannot be readily dismissed as work-shy, feckless, lazy, undeserving or any of the other negative discourses of 'the poor' in the UK.'

'The political debate around work has been neutralised as all the major parties agree that work is a sustainable route out of poverty. However I would argue that only sustainable work is a route out of poverty; i.e. decent work with career development

opportunities. Unfortunately, due to market-based deregu-
lation of UK labour market and labour relations, too many
households (remember, the majority of poor households in the
UK have at least one member in work) become trapped in low-
paid work. For too many, entry level work has no exit strategy!'

'New Labour changed the landscape of employment protection legislation when in power. For example the introduction
of Working Tax Credits, whilst to be applauded on one level
for raising the incomes of some of the lowest paid, also created a system which disincentivises those who attempt to
work their way out of poverty.'

'This is because working longer hours or moving to a
slightly better-paying job to move out of poverty is penal-
ized by the double whammy of increased tax liabilities and
reduced tax credits payments. This can result in effective marginal tax rates of up to 70%; i.e. 70p in the pound is lost to this
poverty trap effect. In this way there is no incentive for workers to work longer hours, move to slightly better-paid jobs or
bargain for better wages. In effect, therefore, subsidising low-
paid employees through Working Tax Credits neutralizes the
effectiveness of individuals' income-maximizing strategies
and of trade union intervention.'

Still worse, for those moving from benefits into work the
effective marginal tax rate can be up to 100%: a £1 reduction
in benefits for every pound earned. This is a major barrier to
work for many households who are branded as work-shy but
whose decision is economically rational. If you only received
a few pounds more for working than not working, would you
choose work?

Debbie's story

Doctor Pattison gives Debbie as an example. Debbie was an outsourced cleaner at Wythenshawe hospital, working for a multi-national corporation contracted to provide 'soft services', such as cleaning and portering. The arrangement is as part of a 35-year Private Finance Initiative (PFI) agreement.

Debbie had to clean 110 bedrooms and several communal areas and corridors in six hours. She had her own designated area as one of a four-woman cleaning team. What made Debbie's situation different was that she was the only employee in her team who'd started after the private company took over. So she wasn't protected by TUPE (the acronym for Transfer of Employment Protection). In a nutshell she worked the same hours, doing the same job, wearing the same uniform and sharing the same cleaning materials as the rest of the team, but her working terms and conditions were inferior. TUPE legislation ensured that the three ladies who'd previously been paid by the NHS didn't have their terms and conditions downgraded. Debbie, as a new starter, was on the private company's terms and conditions. In practice what this meant was that, whilst they were all paid the same (£5.88 per hour), Debbie didn't get any sick pay and was entitled to fewer holidays.

Put yourself in the private company's shoes. I'd guess it was a competitive tender and price played a significant part in their winning the contract. The principle cost of any cleaning contract is staff, so the only way to improve profitability is to squeeze the terms and conditions where you can, and demand more work from the existing teams by not replacing staff who leave or are off sick. The private company did just what their competitors would have done in a similar situation. As night follows day this is the inevitable knock-on effect on some of our lowest paid workers when public services are outsourced to the private sector. It is front-line staff, such as Debbie, who bear the brunt of the new, 'more efficient' delivery model.

So let's look at it from Debbie's perspective. Her work was dirty, hard and very important for the patients' health and smooth running of the hospital, but cleaning is also an unskilled, low-paid job. Labour economics tells us that wages represent the productive value of one's work and so people are highly paid because their work is deemed to have a high value to the economy. Those on low pay have little productive value. With that in mind, how do you put a value on cleaning a hospital?

Debbie was paid £5.88 per hour which was above the national minimum (at the time £5.35) but, though she worked full shifts, she didn't earn enough to meet her basic needs. After rent, bills and transport Debbie struggled to buy enough food every week. She bought economy brands and relied on things that filled her up rather than anything more healthy and nutritious. She rarely socialised. She gave up her one and only social outlet – playing football – because she could not afford the travel and match fees.

Debbie took pride in her work and believed she deserved to be paid more, or at least receive the same terms as her co-workers. With more money she could afford better food, a social life, or some new clothes. However, these basic requirements in twenty-first century Britain were out of her reach. She shared a poorly insulated three-bedroom house with her mum and three siblings. Her two younger sisters (14 and 8) shared a bed in the room where she also slept, giving her brother and mum their own space. As a fully employed young adult, moving out wasn't an option – she couldn't afford to move and her family couldn't afford for her to move out.

You can say Debbie should have known better or tried harder, but let's briefly consider her life to date. Her mum used to work at the hospital but was on long-term sick leave due to a bad back (all too common in this type of work) and depression (brought on by a life in poverty and a low-paid, dead-end job), so she is now the main breadwinner. She wanted to carry on in education and go to university but she had to leave school at sixteen to put some money into the household. One of her only routes out of poverty was ended. She is now in a low paid job with no prospect of escaping from this end of the labour market. Like her mum she has already had considerable periods of time off work with stress and depression.

The most poignant thing about Debbie is that almost any one of us could have ended up in this position if our lives had taken a slightly different turn.

Child poverty

Possibly nothing defines the true values of a society as the way in which it treats its children and young people. How it teaches them values such as kindness, compassion and generosity, as much as maths and history. How it teaches the importance of service, contribution and respect as much as forging an individual, self-centred path in life. And how it cares for them.

How do kids in the UK fare today? In 2008, Unicef reported that the UK is one of the very worst places to be a child. We're bottom of their 'children's well-being' league table across 21 industrialised countries. Poverty is rampant. One in four children live below the poverty line. Around 1.8 million children live in workless households. And two-thirds of these are lone parent households.

Incredibly England actually has a Children's Commissioner, Professor Sir Al Anysley-Green. Anysley-Green is both effective and compassionate. He has commented 'We are turning out a generation of young people who are unhappy, unhealthy, engaging in risky behaviour, who have poor relationships with their family and peers, who have low expectations and don't feel safe.' Yet our schools focus on academic achievement.

We also have an Independent Commission on Social Mobility. Their report, published in January 2009, put the problem of being a child in our country succinctly:

'Britain is a society of persistent inequality. The life-chances of children in Britain today remain heavily dependent on the circumstances of their birth ... children born to poorer families have less favourable outcomes across every sphere of life. Inequality creates barriers to upward mobility. These barriers impede progress at all stages: from before birth into the early years, through primary and secondary school and into the adult labour market. They are revealed in the measurable gaps in educational attainment, in differential employment opportunities and in health inequalities.'

'Who ends up with good or bad health is not just a matter of luck. There is a relationship between health and wealth pertinent to social mobility: those who suffer poor health as children or as adults are less likely to be upwardly mobile; those who start life in a low social class are more likely to experience poor health. Despite the huge medical and public health advances of the past fifty years, health inequalities persist between those at the bottom and the top of the social stratum. These inequalities begin before birth and continue throughout the life course. A child from the lowest social class is more likely to: be born too early, be born small; have a mother who smokes and grow up to be a smoker him/herself; die or be injured in a childhood accident; become a young parent; suffer chronic illness in adulthood, and, eventually, to die several years earlier than his/her better off peers. The gulf in healthy life expectancy across the UK is deeply shocking and cannot be tolerated.'

'Poor health impacts on educational attainment, employment and income, thereby further decreasing the likelihood of a child born into poverty attaining upward mobility.'

Under ten years old . . . and no future

Primary school is many children's first glimpse of a world outside their home. The first real opportunity to learn how to mix with other kids, to begin to cope with life, to play, add up and subtract, to read. Here, tomorrow's people are being made, future mums and dads, tradesmen and women, entrepreneurs, career politicians, businessmen.

I have travelled to the Northwest, encouraged to visit a primary school with an inspirational head teacher, who is working on education's front line. I am visiting a town which rose to prosperity during the industrial revolution, but where the traditional employment base has been in decline for several decades. It is now one of the poorest towns in Britain, in the top six percent of most deprived boroughs. The number of its working-age population claiming incapacity benefit, at thirteen percent, is almost double the national average.

Unsurprisingly, local educational achievement reflects these disadvantages and its educational track record is abysmal. Three of the five secondary schools are in the bottom five percent of the national league tables for adding value between the end of Key Stage 2 and the end of Key Stage 4, and two are in special measures. In the centre of town 15% of properties are empty, 27% classified as unfit to live in. Four in ten households rely on some form of state benefit. Poverty is a serious problem, as are ill health, drug and alcohol misuse, depression, domestic violence and crime.

This is a modern school, the result of a merger between four smaller primary schools. It is bright, warm and bustling, with 300 noisy boys and girls aged from three to eleven and an equally energetic, mostly young, teaching staff of sixteen, led by a remarkably warm and enthusiastic head called Wendy. She knows everyone by name and gives all the outward signs of being powered by several Duracell batteries.

At first sight all looks good and well, but this school has the dubious cachet of being the 150th 'most challenging school in Britain'. Its catchment area comprises neighbourhoods that almost all fall into the bottom five percent in terms of socio-economic indicators. Most parents are on benefits. The surrounding housing is poor. Half the homes are boarded-up and shops are scarce.

The majority of children come from single-parent families. Sixty-eight percent are eligible for free school meals. A significant majority arrive having experienced some kind of emotional trauma. Many witness domestic violence; most come from families with alcohol or drug related problems; many have parents with mental health problems. I am not using 'many' and 'most' lightly. This is a fact. And parental background is critical: by the time these children are five years old, they will have spent more hours with their parents than they will spend at school throughout their entire education.

Of the hundred and fifty families represented at the school, twelve are known to be in work. In one of the merged schools, all the children can be traced back to just two families. They thought they were cousins, but are in fact half-brothers and -sisters. Third-generation unemployment is common, which means that there is no history or memory of work whatsoever in many of the families. Employment isn't an aspiration because the kids have no reference point. 'What do you want to be when you grow up?' I ask. 'A man.' 'When you're a man, what do you think you'll do?' 'Go down the Post (office).' . . . where the benefit money is paid out. Job done.

Given their backgrounds it is a miracle that many of the children make it to school each day at all. When I asked Wendy what her measurements of success were she thought for a moment and then, in all seriousness, replied that in some cases success was the fact that the child was still alive. And then she went on to relate the story of the starfish.

THE STORY OF THE STARFISH

A man was walking along a beach. The sun was shining and it was a beautiful day. In the distance he could see a young boy going back and forth between the surf's edge and the beach. Then he noticed hundreds of starfish stranded on the sand. The boy was hurling them one by one back into the sea.

The man was stuck by the apparent futility of the task. There were far too many starfish to save. But, as he approached, the boy continued picking up starfish one by one and throwing them into the surf.

'You must be crazy' said the man when he reached him. 'There are thousands of miles of beach covered with starfish. You can't possibly make a difference.' The boy held the man's gaze. He then stooped down, picked up one more starfish and threw it back into the ocean. He turned back to the man and smiled, 'it made a difference to that one!'

....

For the children themselves, going to school has some advantages even if the purpose isn't always clear. It's warm, you get breakfast and lunch, some of your friends are there, a couple of the teachers are magic and huggable.

And while teachers join up to teach, they can't operate here unless they know each child and their family circumstances well. They must learn that the real reason one child is not at school every day is because her mother is clinically depressed and can't get out of bed to bring her in. Another's aggression is learned from witnessing domestic violence at home on a regular basis. When I visited the school the Child Learning Mentor – the key person who works to resolve family issues impacting the children – had been off work for six weeks with stress; probably because ten people doing that job would still not have been enough.

A boy of nine lives with his mum and two younger siblings, three and six-months old. Mum was fourteen when he was born and struggles with post-natal depression. She is unable to cope with his behaviour at home, is violent, bullies her other children, hates the boy and regularly threatens to put him into care.

Another child has been excluded twice after assaulting a teacher. His mum has both overdosed and attempted suicide by hanging. After the latter, she was admitted to A&E but discharged herself with the drip still in her arm.

This is the life experience for these three hundred children on a daily and weekly basis. Their reality; what they know. Their peer group will shape their life and their expectations in a similar manner to prisoners who learn all they wish to about crime by being locked up together. There is a desperate shortage of role models, and only occasional flashes of hope of escape into a better universe. If you spend a few hours amongst these children then press an imaginary fast-forward button it is very difficult to arrive at an optimistic, happy ending. In ten years time these very small people will have survived their education and one or two may have landed on their feet. By then we may also be debating what to do with the fourth generation of unemployed who, finding themselves deserted by cutbacks at 'the Post', make contact outside their neighbourhood for a weekly visit for cash to a hole in the wall. Completely out of sight and mind.

This is what Unicef meant when they implied that the UK is one of the most miserable places in the western world to be a child. This is not something that happens just in 'the north', or areas of extreme deprivation. Look around and you will find similar scenarios in any town or city from London to Liverpool, Norwich to Newcastle.

In many ways these children are on a par with the street children of Delhi. Each day is a survival course.

So now you know

13.5 million in poverty is almost too big a problem. Try to mention it and I usually get an embarrassed silence or a blank stare; sometimes a reflex denial. It has to be said that 'figures' induce stupor. If a hungry woman and child appeared on your door step and asked for food, or money to buy some, you would probably help them and it would be easy to grasp the impact you were having. But thirteen million puts the issue well beyond our grasp – or our stereotypes of gangs, pregnant teenagers, and the unemployed. It makes it a central issue which is both hard to take in and really uncomfortable from the cosiness of a warm living room and your own bed.

If we are to move from passivity to action, we need to be brave enough to get out more and experience at first hand what's going on. To move from being the largely passive recipients of edited TV and press highlights that don't intrude too much, to a place which is more thought-provoking and uncomfortable. Even if you work full time, you need only invest a day, maybe less, to check out how the other half live.

All politicians must know about this shocking poverty, and the impact it is having our schools and indeed in our society. All media editors must know it too. But the majority of the public don't realise the seriousness of it. It is a national scandal almost on a par with Dickensian times, only there is no Dickens to draw our attention to the poor and the workhouse.

For those of you who believe that charity should begin at home – here is your chance.

Take the first step

Learn as much as you can about the real poverty in your own neighbourhood. You will be shocked – within half a mile or a mile of where you live there will be many cases of real poverty and hardship. Just look.

Listen. Many people get very bad breaks in life. They are made redundant, lose their homes, separate from a once loved one, miss out on part of their education, are abused, become depressed, drop into addiction, and much more. Resist the temptation to 'transmit', be compassionate and understanding. Be quiet, listen, learn and don't believe the nonsense people tell you. Or, sometimes, that you tell you.

Be the little boy – and throw just one starfish back into the sea. Make a difference, if only to one person.

Resolve to offer practical support to those who are dealing with the most vulnerable and marginalised groups in our society, in any way you can. From offering hands on help at your local school to pressurising your local councillors and MP, or even becoming a local councillor or school governor.

Sign up to 38 Degrees. 38 Degrees is an online campaign group that encourages members take simple, powerful actions to weigh in at critical moments 'when our values are at stake and we can make a difference'. Sometimes they act online, like signing a petition or emailing an MP or corporate leader. Sometimes they act offline, like calling an MP or visiting a surgery. **www.38degrees.org.uk**

6. Generosity at home

'That best portion of a good man's life, his little nameless, unremembered acts of kindness and of love.'

WILLIAM WORDSWORTH

Help others, help ourselves

Our existence isn't just about money or material wealth, but about living generous and fulfilling lives. Given the choice between an inward, acquisitive, worried existence centred on self, and a generous, open and engaged life centred on others, the decision should be easy. A generous life is a happier life. And Act 1, Scene 1 of a more generous life is simply to start being more generous towards those closest to us; our family, friends, work colleagues and even – possibly most importantly – those on the outer edge of our social radar.

Everyone has it within them to become a significant and powerful force for good, no matter what life has thrown at them. Some people are natural listeners and have great empathy, the sort of people who are always there for us when we need them. The rest of us can be like them if we just pause for breath and think. And when we start to focus on others, we find a sense of purpose that gives us a sense of proportion and balance against all our own struggles and difficulties.

There's a course for practically everything these days – how to build self-confidence, set goals, meditate, achieve, raise your family, care for your baby. You name it and you'll find it. But every course that involves relationships has at its core similar principles. In relationships, everyone is different. To get through difficult times (in marriage, with your kids, at work, parenting teenagers, supporting people with mental health problems, dealing with difficult behaviour) you need to understand that difference and listen to whoever is talking to you, reflect back to them that you have understood (you may know what they should do, but the advice is to keep quiet at this stage) and only when you really understand help them come up with their solutions – not yours.

Volunteers at the Samaritans are trained not to give advice, but to listen. When the Reverend Chad Varah founded the charity in 1953, his plan was to give people who were lonely and suicidal the benefit of his professional counselling. So many people queued to see him that he got a whole load of volunteers to make cups of tea and chat until those queuing could be ushered into his presence. And, much to his surprise, cups of tea and someone to chat to meant that most people received the help they needed without seeing him at all. Over fifty years later, the Samaritans has eighty paid staff and 17,500 volunteers.

Peer mentoring works equally well because mentors can say 'I've been there, felt that and survived. I know what you're going through and I'm here for you.' What is the purpose of life? In part it is to be there for other people who need you. Sometimes that, in itself, is enough to give purpose to a day.

Put yourself in someone else's shoes rather than banging on about your life, your worries and your triumphs and disasters. Make time for others; listen before you speak or suggest a solution; remember that your perspective may not be relevant to the person you're speaking to. It's their life; empathise. Focus on the person you're talking to, resist the temptation to broadcast.

You won't become a saint overnight, or get a mention in the New Year's Honours list (not yet anyway!), but in deciding to help others you will change and enhance your own life as much as theirs, for many years ahead. Isn't that an amazing thought?

ACTION
....

What we think, or what we know, or what we believe is in the end of little consequence; the only consequence is what we do.

John Ruskin
....

It is deeply rewarding to engage our gentle and caring side in helping others. To show love, kindness, thoughtfulness and empathy. Our best part, the real us that can get buried underneath the hustle, stress and problems of everyday life. The part that is moved by music, cries during soppy films, loves good friends and is actually touched by the plight of others in this country and around the world. As the Dalai Lama said: 'If you want to be happy, practise compassion. If you want others to be happy, practise compassion.'

How is Everybody?

We have cars which isolate us, TVs and X-boxes to entertain us, we text people not in the room rather than pay attention to those who are. Many homes have no space to share a family meal around a table (despite research which shows this is important) and there are families where generations live continents apart. We take a new job; we move away. It's all too easy to lose touch – we know so many people and yet really know so few. In just a few months jobs can be lost, careers surge, or a terminal illness can strike. Teens often speak a different language from their parents and almost inevitably from their grandparents. 'I find it depressing', muttered a contact assessing juvenile mental health in the UK , 'that charities seem to be picking up a whole load of stuff that families and friends would have done a generation or so ago. And they can never replace what a family could have given in love and care.' Quite.

Generosity should start with your family, friends and work colleagues, and extend to people you vaguely know, or know by sight only, whom you might otherwise pass with a nod or a passing smile. Your actions and behaviour influence everyone you're in contact with on a regular basis. People close to you need your help, so before you start 'saving the world', pause and think of those closest to you: start practising in-reach before you try outreach.

Why don't you set some time aside from your busy, stressful, fascinating or boring life to think about other people and their lives? Put a decent amount of time in your diary within the next seven days. Try to make sure that you don't have to be somewhere, or do something, for a couple of hours. Because this is just the beginning of what will turn out to be a really interesting, involving and positive experience.

Choose a quiet spot where you won't be interrupted, turn off your mobile and find somewhere where no one will pop in to disturb you; a room at home; a favourite spot in the garden; a rug beneath a tree or beside a river; a bench looking out to sea; a local church. Have with you a pad of paper, a pen and your address or phone book to prompt ideas (OK, maybe you have to turn your mobile back on to go through your latest contact list). Settle down with just yourself and your thoughts.

Your mission is to think about the people you know from *their* perspective. Try to imagine yourself in their shoes. This can be quite difficult, especially trying to override your pre-conceptions and judgements of other people, their behaviour and mannerisms. How is everybody? It is quite extraordinary how focusing your mind on another person's life for five minutes will give you a new insight into their world and some of the situations they are facing. We are all so busy and so concerned about our own lives, our own triumphs and concerns, that the problems of even our closest friends often pass us by completely.

Are they happy? Pretty content and on good form? Is it their birthday soon (and are you about to forget it?) or are they about to celebrate something? Are they going for a job interview or have they just started a new job; taken an important exam or just passed one; moved home or retired? Is it time to congratulate them on something or wish them good luck? Are you totally out of touch? Ring, email or write a quick note. Now!

It takes a quiet moment to get through the bravado. For people to open up and admit they are finding life a bit tough. Perhaps they are unhappy, stressed or not very well physically; facing serious challenges at work or having problems with a relationship. Are they lonely or having a difficult time financially? What sorts of problems are they facing?

They might be seriously depressed. One in six people in this country will suffer from some form of mental illness and depression is on the rise. I suffered a very nasty attack of clinical depression in my mid-forties and fortunately, with some excellent medical help, exercise, prayer and wonderful support from all my family and friends, I made a complete recovery. At my lowest ebb, when I had become deeply vulnerable and incapable of sensible thought or behaviour, the generosity of my family and friends was immeasurable, and very loving. By being quite open about it I suddenly found significant numbers of people who were fellow sufferers, most of whom had never dared to tell anyone who didn't need to know.

Everyone has their own problems and we are all insecure, however confident we may seem. Your mission is to think about those closest to you and the challenges they face and then do something to show that you care about their situation. Generosity of thought followed by generosity of action.

Make a time now or you will put it off. Remember, it is the little things you do that really help and procrastination doesn't help at all. No one is aware they are in your thoughts unless you touch base and tell them.

Generosity to family

'Oh, do we have to?' you groan. Challenging this one, isn't it? Think about your ageing parents, your in-laws, the sister who's moved away (with her very dull husband), your brother (with whom you have nothing in common), your cousin (whom you fell out with when he/she behaved impossibly at a family wedding). You may think it is just your family, but in my experience everyone has some no-go areas with their nearest and dearest.

In an ideal world, our relationships with those closest to us would be the warmest and most loving. But you don't have to be a psychologist to realise that those we know best we often judge most harshly. We see their questionable habits, weaknesses and sometimes nasty little ways. As they do ours. We can hold grudges for years. The younger sibling is always expected to play second fiddle to the elder, even when they're approaching retirement themselves. Old habits die hard.

And, of course, the really depressing fact is that if you have a problem or a dispute with a member of your family – whatever the cause, whoever did what to whom and whoever was right or wrong – it is hard to forgive. We have all heard: 'I will never speak to him/her again.' My father wasn't really on speaking terms with his brother; my father-in-law had a similar situation with his brother. I don't think either set had a lot in common, but it did seem an awful waste.

Many years back my wife and I went on a marriage course. It seemed like a good idea at the time and we didn't go because our marriage was on the rocks, we went to learn. The course was excellent and it reaffirmed that we know what we're meant to do, but that it is all too easy to forget. Give each other one to one time; listen to each other; forgive. The same applies to any long-term relationship. 'Love is an active verb' we were reminded, ' you need to make an effort.'

Generosity to Friends

From quiet homes and first beginning, out to the undiscovered ends, there's nothing worth the wear of winning, but laughter and the love of friends

Hilaire Belloc

How are your friends? The really good friends you haven't seen for ages, but would love to catch up with again. The people who you know well, and those you would like to get to know better. Where are they? When did you last see them? Are they OK or do they need a hug?

Perhaps you hardly see the friends you really like, your best friends, since they moved, got married or began a new job. Proper friendships, the people who have been through lots with you, whom you care most about and in turn care most about you, are invaluable.

Wasting time with a friend is not wasting time. Swapping news and just being together for no particular purpose is a true blessing and part of what friendships are all about. Put some time aside to make sure you catch up. It is more important than an extra hour at the office. Maybe this is a time for a 'social cull', or at least time to focus on spending your spare time with people you actually like as opposed to being continuously sociable.

One of my friends used to divide the people she knew into 'day time' and 'night time' friends. It was her way of separating all those nice, chatty people you meet during the day – at school or at work – from those you would actually invite home for supper, a chat and a drink. But perhaps it is too easy to dismiss 'problem' people as people you are no longer close to? You could try your hand at Desert Island Friends. In Radio 4's Desert Island Discs celebrities are cast away on a desert island with the Bible, the complete works of Shakespeare, one luxury and eight favourite pieces of music. In Desert Island Friends, instead of your eight favourite pieces of music, you can take eight friends with you, including family members. It can be a very sobering game. Most people can't actually name eight, and many wouldn't take members of their own family.

Generosity at Work

You spend a great deal of time with your colleagues at work. Some are a laugh, others seem really friendly but you don't see much of them during the day; some you wouldn't trust further than you can throw them, others are hugely ambitious and don't have a life; some have been there for most of their adult lives and live for the weekends, or to pursue an eccentric hobby!

Grab an internal phone list. Go through it and think for a moment about your colleagues' lives and what you know of them. Perhaps go to lunch with someone you usually wouldn't, or have a drink with them after work. You will be pleasantly surprised by how often people's lives and interests 'outside work' will make them more approachable, and reveal them as fellow humans! And you as a better colleague.

Management team-building games can provide a common framework where surprising one-to-one conversations can happen. My cousin told me of a management programme whose methodology was to take people out of their comfort zone, facilitating communication and understanding between colleagues at a much more profound level. A close colleague of his talked about the fact that she had a very traumatic upbringing, including being abused. He was extremely moved, and his point to me was that he would never have known this without 'getting out of the office'.

THE MILLWRIGHT WHO DIED

In the furniture industry of the 1920s the machines of most factories were not run by electric motors, but by pulleys from a central drive shaft. The central drive shaft was run by steam.

The steam engine got its steam from the boiler. The boiler, in our case, got its fuel from the sawdust and other waste coming out of the machine room – a beautiful cycle.

The millwright was the person who oversaw that cycle and on whom the entire activity of the operation depended. He was the key person.

One night the millwright died.

My father, a young manager at the time, did not particularly know what he should do but he thought he should go and visit the family. He went to the house and was invited to join the family in the living room. There was some awkward conversation – the kind with which many of us are familiar.

The widow asked my father if it would be all right if she read aloud some poetry. Naturally he agreed. She went into another room, came back with a bound book, and for many minutes read selected pieces of beautiful poetry. When she was finished, my father commented on how beautiful the poetry was and asked who wrote it. She replied that her husband, the millwright, was the poet.

It is now nearly sixty years since the millwright died and my father and many of us at Herman Miller continue to wonder:

was he a poet who did a millwright's work, or was he a millwright who wrote poetry?

An extract from *Leadership is an Art* **– by Max De Pree, CEO of Herman Miller**

....

Just as there was more to the millwright than his job (see box opposite), there is more to most people than we first see, or choose to see: often because we don't actually care or bother to find out. We make assumptions based on our personal perspectives. We ask 'what do you do?' not 'who are you?' We judge people by their dress and – often temporary - status, rather than valuing their experience and wisdom. We fail to see them in the round.

Generosity towards people you hardly know

We all tend to like people who are similar to ourselves, or whom we admire, and spend most of our time with them. There is nothing wrong with this, but for a while I would like you to think of the people you don't know as well, wouldn't normally socialise with or even think of talking to – people who are quite simply on the edge of your social radar screen, those you might even think boring. (One definition of a drinks party is 'a gathering where everyone present is a crashing bore except you'!)

My mother-in-law, Eleanor, always insisted that no-one was boring if you asked them about themselves and then listened to them. Rubbish, I would tell her. Some people are as dull as ditchwater. But I learnt that she was completely right and no one is boring if you persevere. People's most interesting subject is themselves. Ask them about their family (good one for parents who are generally besotted by their children) or their work (some people do very dull jobs, but at least by asking them about it you learn about that area of life).

I always ask people: 'What do you do when you are not being dynamic?' followed by: 'Are you a lethal tennis player, a frustrated opera singer, an obsessed fisherman?' Which leads to mild laughter and to surprising places. Touch on a person's interests and you will have their attention for ages. You may find yourself going through entire parties without anyone asking you anything about your own life.

How to be a Good Samaritan

Who do you know who is generally shunned, politely ignored and avoided by yourself and others? Those people who have a very hard life and a terribly lonely time. Those people who need a kind word or act to lift their spirits. Those people we label problem people, dull or difficult or simply write off as no-hopers. The people who face discrimination because they're disabled, have lost the plot mentally, look different, or are easy to make fun of.

Everyone has heard of the Biblical parable of the Good Samaritan. Jesus tells a lawyer that he should love his neighbour as much as he loves himself. 'Who is my neighbour?' replies the man (they can be quite pedantic, these lawyers).

Let's remind ourselves of the parable:

A man was travelling from Jerusalem to Jericho when he was attacked by robbers, who stripped and beat him, and left leaving him half dead. The next person to arrive was a priest who saw the half dead man and passed by on the other side of the road. Then came a Levite. He did exactly the same. The third passer-by was a Samaritan. When he saw the man he was moved with compassion, came to him and treated and bound up his wounds. Then he put him on his own animal and brought him to an inn so that he could take care of him properly. When the Samaritan had to leave the next day, he gave the innkeeper two days money to look after the injured man's needs with instructions to carry on doing whatever was necessary to look after him, and assurances that if more money was needed, the Samaritan would pay the extra on his return journey.

Having told the parable, Jesus asked the lawyer which of the three had been a good neighbour to the injured man. 'He who showed mercy'. 'Then go and do likewise.'

One of the key points of the parable is the contrast. The priest and the Levite were religious leaders (Levites helping priests in the temple) and put their self-interests first. Touching the poor man risked making them unclean and so they left him to die. The Samaritan was one of society's outcasts and wouldn't have come from that neighbourhood; so not a neighbour by any definition. Yet he stopped and helped. He bound the man's wounds, dressed them with oil and wine, put him on his donkey, paid two days of his wages to the inn-keeper and promised to pay more when he returned. He was looked upon as the lowest of the low but he acted. Those who should and could have helped didn't. The unmentioned question the priest and the Levite asked themselves was: *'If I stop to help this man, what will happen to me?'* The Samaritan reversed the question and asked: *'If I do not stop to help this man what will happen to him?'* The parable is so well known that academics all over the world examine 'The Samaritan Paradox.' Is the motivation to help in part because we expect reciprocity? And therefore selfish after all? But the Samaritan of the parable was not from the area and already outcast. He was helping a stranger, who intriguingly is the only person in the story who is not identified. Reciprocity doesn't seem to be part of the story. This man obviously needed help but he wasn't capable of asking for it.

Now own up. How many times have you deliberately 'passed by on the other side'.

Have you ignored someone's plea for help, or knew someone who was having a difficult time but avoided asking them about it for fear of 'getting too close'. Have you avoided someone because you see 'homeless', 'alcoholic', 'waster' – not the person? You might have hurried on with your own life, because you were slightly scared and anyway you are very busy, and someone else will step in.

Take the first step

It really is the little, unexpected acts of generosity that people remember and are touched by. They take thought and a bit of effort but invariably cost very little. Little things matter a lot.

Put some time aside in your diary. Think about individual members of your family. How are they? Ring a couple of them that you haven't spoken to recently and ask them. How are your friends? The people you really love, admire, trust, laugh with, have known since you were at school? Arrange to meet to catch up – even if they live in another part of the country or another country altogether.

Think about work. Who do you not know much about at work, but have often been curious about? Or felt sorry for? One of my friends was prompted by this idea to ask his secretary out for lunch – she was very surprised but they had fun and learned more about how each ticked.

Cheer someone up. Who do you know who is having a difficult time? Make space to talk to them, ask them how they are, and encourage them. Most of all listen!

Be a Good Samaritan. Go out of your way to help someone you don't know at all. This week. Quietly. Do any of the people who surround you in your life, need help? What is the best thing you can do to help them? What could you do today, in the next few days, or when you see them next, that would help them in a practical way and show them that you care about them?

Be secretly generous! Buy a book token and place it in a best-seller, so the next person who picks it up can have it for free; hand a fiver to the flower seller and ask them to give flowers to someone who would appreciate it; secretly treat the people in the queue behind you to their cappuccino, or cinema ticket; or pay for a stranger's meal in a restaurant.

Spread the work of The Kindness Offensive beyond London. Or join in if you're in London. It's about having fun and sharing – distributing free tickets, food, chocolates, kitchen equipment etc directly to people who need it. Just before Christmas 2008 volunteers handed out 3,500 hampers and over 12,000 toys via different charities and community groups. On Pancake Day they give away over half a million pancakes!
www.thekindnessoffensive.com

Commit a Random Acts of Kindness. Be inspired by the movement's website. They've a suggestion for every day: hold a door open for someone with a buggy; help a kid with their homework; let another driver go first; pick up some litter; pay a compliment to the person at the supermarket checkout. Or just smile and be nice to people! **www.actsofkindness.org**

Join the organ donor register. If everyone in the UK did there would be enough healthy organs for everyone, saving three lives a day, as well as big savings on the NHS advertising budget. **www.organdonation.nhs.uk**

Sign up to give blood. Today. As they say on the website, 96% of us rely on the 4% who do. **www.blood.co.uk**

Let someone keep the change.

7. Generous communities

Ask not what your country can do for you
– ask what you can do for your country

JOHN F. KENNEDY, INAUGURAL ADDRESS
JANUARY 20ᵀᴴ 1961

Your country needs YOU!

Many of us have lost confidence in our politicians, and
are even more sceptical of our bankers. The blame
game is in full swing. It is difficult to quote meaningful figures here because the outlook is changing every week, so by
the time you read this the detail will be out of date. The big
picture, sadly, won't change that quickly. The money borrowed
in such enormous sums, to keep the banks and financial systems intact and the global economy out of intensive care, will
have to be repaid. Our national deficit is currently running at
historic levels. A quick look at the official figures is very sobering. According to the Office for National Statistics, in just five
fun-packed years of so called 'growth', UK government debt

almost doubled to £950 billion at the end of 2009 (that's 68% of GDP – gross domestic product) and our annual deficit was £159 billion, 11.4% of GDP.

That's a load of money, any way you care to count it. Debt of any kind has to be repaid one day. Politicians of all parties, economists and the financial wizards who created this shocking situation in the first place are all agreed – there are going to be severe cuts in government expenditure until at least 2014.

However many 'efficiencies' are found, this will hurt. There will be public sector pay freezes and job cuts and probably significant tax increases. A perfect storm for the growth of poverty.

The light at the end of the tunnel . . . is that of the oncoming train

Translated into plain English this means that any dreams we still have of the state as answer to all our ills, are castles in the air. The social fabric of Britain is about to have a heart attack. Cuts in public services mean cuts in funding to our schools, hospitals and social services. Despite efficiency savings, already stressed services will be even more constrained.

The Catch 22 is, the deeper the cuts bite, the greater the need for the services being withdrawn. More of us are suffering from anxiety and depression, with the upward trend predicted to continue. The knock-on impact on employers and the NHS is easy to foresee. We all know about our rising elderly population, who will not be cheap to care for. I am going to be one of them! The prison population grew by 68% between 1995 and 2009, to 83,900, and is forecast to reach

93,000 by 2015. A costly business that many would argue is also counterproductive. Given the choice between early intervention for school-children who are in danger of going off the rails and ending up as a prison statistic, or building new prisons to house our criminals, it seem likely the kids will lose out. The St Giles Trust have reported that 55% of prisoners reoffend and estimate the costs of reoffending at £11 billion a year. Whatever the figures, the social costs are huge, both to the victims and to the perpetrators who have mucked up their lives. The budget might once have stretched to prevent some kid's downward spiral into a grim adulthood but, in the current climate, relying on the government to offer solutions to society's needs just isn't going to work.

The British economy shrank 4.5% in 2009 and living standards were back at 2005 levels. Most of us will cope, though we may not like it, but inevitably it is the poorest sections of society – children, the unemployed, single parents, people who are sick, disabled or elderly – who will suffer disproportionately. Groups which combine to form the majority of our society.

Governments, of whatever political persuasion, cannot keep pace with every pressing social, medical and cultural need because the only place to get such enormous resources from is us, the tax-payers. But most of us want to pay less tax, not more, and promising tax rises is a sure way for a party to fail to get elected.

At first sight this might seem like a cause for national despair, a cast-iron case for leaving the country, emigrating to China or India, and the subject matter for hours of gloomy conversation about the final demise of 'once-Great Britain': 'will the last person to leave these islands please turn the lights out?'.

But in fact the whole sorry situation offers us a wonderful chance to regain a bit of spirit in adversity, and to show that we care about the people with whom we share this small island. There is an opportunity to create great change by doing small things: involving ourselves in the warp and weft of community life; not accepting the status quo, but taking matters into our own hands. To actively engage in generosity, to become involved with and get stuck into helping our own communities, to undertake and carry out ourselves the numerous small but important tasks that are going to be abandoned while our Social Services, NHS, education system and more are carpet-bombed by accountants.

Getting involved

The good news is that our villages, towns and cities are just that, ours, to become involved in, to change and to improve. They are full of wonderful and imaginative community groups, social enterprises and a host of local organisations all working quietly to make life better. The even better news is that there is also a wonderfully strong charitable sector throughout the UK – 182,000 organisations at the last count. Charities and charitable work are part of the DNA of British society and you'll find most of the major national charities, as well as many smaller local ones, in every town and city throughout the country.

The recession is taking its toll on them too. The largest funder of the UK charity sector in the recent past has been the government, encouraging charities to pitch against NHS trusts and private and public companies to provide essential services.

At their best charities are innovators and entrepreneurs. They are often established because someone has become incensed by an injustice and is determined to do something about it. They carry on because they are determined to overcome the odds and find better solutions. They do a huge amount to inform government policy, as well as getting on with the job of looking after some of the most marginalised groups of society: children whom everyone else has given up on, offenders, victims of domestic violence. Research into brain injury, Alzheimer's, Parkinson's, multiple sclerosis and many more life-threatening conditions would be nowhere near as advanced without the efforts of and funding from charities. They connect us with a cause, handle the bureaucracy where it (inevitably) exists, lobby hard to obtain central and regional government funding and fight with their supporters on everyone's behalf for a more even playing field.

Where would our countryside be without charities like the National Trust, RSPB or even thousands of village fetes in aid of the local church restoration fund? Our culture without public-supported institutions like the Tate, the Natural History Museum and the Edinburgh Festival? To say nothing of our ability and willingness to support overseas crises through the Disasters Emergency Committee, Unicef, Oxfam and the Red Cross.

There is a charity for every cause, sometimes several competing charities, caring for every possible social and physical need. If you are not already formally or informally linked to one or more of these causes, now is the time to do something about it. You might be surprised at the number of people you know who spend a few hours a week doing something useful to help others, even if they already have a demanding day job. Quietly, on a regular basis and without making a fuss.

There are over a million charity trustees for a start. University Freshers' Week stalls include a whole section on volunteering. There's Volunteering England (www.volunteering.org.uk), a £5 million charity whose sole purpose is to help us volunteer, or Do-It (www.do-it.org.uk) a national database and website putting young people in contact with suitable local opportunities. Twenty-three million of us claim to be actively involved in volunteering in our own communities: many of your friends and work colleagues will already be involved in fundraising, helping out as a carer or mentor, acting as a trustee or governor, or just pitching in wherever they are needed. And, just as likely, someone you know is being looked after by someone working with a charity, even though they may never tell you.

Quite apart from the benefit to others, volunteering often provides training and can be a good leg up into a paid job. When we volunteer through charities to support their beneficiaries we rely on their expertise to set the framework for us. That framework usually involves elements such as learning how to keep any relationship on a friendly but professional basis, avoiding the danger of creating dependence, making sure volunteers who help vulnerable adults or children are CRB checked and, in more sensitive work like the Samaritans, supporting the volunteers themselves through what may be traumatic experiences.

THE FOOD CHAIN

A friend told me this story: 'Once, when our three children were very, very young (three under the age of three), a friend rang in the middle of the afternoon and said, "Don't cook supper. I'm bringing some round at 5 pm" We waited with great anticipation. Sure enough, on the pip of five, she appeared with a chicken casserole, potatoes and salad. Supper was handed over to us on the doorstep. This gift really touched us and has inspired me to do the same. A cake or supper – unsolicited – makes people's hearts soft. It's simple, unexpected and it works. Surprise is definitely a key element!'

Where I live there is now an established neighbourhood Food Chain. People volunteer to cook and deliver meals on an informal rota to anyone in the local community that their radar is alerted to. Someone might be convalescing from an operation, in the middle of chemotherapy, looking after a sick child or a new baby, suffering a bereavement – whatever it is that's making life difficult, the wonders of email make it easy to alert the group, and enough people put their hands up to cook, contact and deliver a meal, often regular meals over several weeks. The group is big enough to provide a continuous stream of 'real' ready meals, packed in foil containers, almost all out-of-the-oven fresh: fish pies, shepherds pies, chicken casseroles, soups, puddings and more.

Many of those helped initially insist they can cope, but in truth they are always touched by the kindness, bowled over by the idea that someone they might not even know has taken the time out to do this for them, and cheered by contact with someone who has set aside some time to brighten up their day. The impact is much greater than just a meal that you haven't had to think about.

And you won't be surprised to learn that the people cooking and delivering all this food enjoy doing it (cooking an extra helping or two is, after all, very little extra effort) and find the whole experience very rewarding. A casual conversation which before may have been 'did you know?' translates quickly into 'we can help'. And it's true that lots of people who need some extra TLC at a variety of levels besides food would never normally broadcast it. As impressive and heart-warming as all this is, what really hits home is the incredible simplicity of the Food Chain. There are enough cooks involved not to over-burden anyone, and it all just 'happens' with the minimum of fuss and drama.

....

Perfection, procrastination and paralysis

We often think about doing something useful locally, knowing that it is good to help other people and do something worthwhile with our lives. We talk about it a great deal but somehow we never get round to it. 'One day, when I have more time . . .' we say. But the time to start giving and being useful is *now*, not tomorrow. If we want to make our country a more civilised place to live, now and for future generations, we can create the greatest change by doing it ourselves. We are the amorphous 'grass roots' who know what's going on and can do something about it. We don't need layers of bureaucracy to find out.

It is time to grab the chance while we can; before people die of loneliness and lack of care because we are too busy. The plain truth is that we have absolutely no guarantee of a tomorrow. The opportunity to help our families, our friends and our communities might vanish completely, while we are 'thinking about it' or 'waiting for more time'. As Peter Melchett, a former director of Greenpeace, has said: ' I prefer the optimism of action to the pessimism of thought'.

So this is a call to action. The government can cut spending, but it is within every individual's power to apply themselves and have a hundred times more impact. We can set an example to our politicians and leaders and demand change – by the people for the people. By making an effort to help others and improve our communities, we also improve our own lives immeasurably.

THE SECRET OF THE SECRET MILLIONAIRE

The Secret Millionaire has become a hit TV programme, with an average audience of 3.5 million. The premise is this: someone who has made several million and lives a comfortable life complete with colour-supplement home and suitable smart car, agrees to spend ten days 'under cover' in one of the UK's poorer towns or cities, during which time they will live off unemployment benefit. Their mission is to search out local social and charitable projects, find out more about them by offering to volunteer, then select some to give cash to. There's a reasonably plausible cover story to explain the presence of a camera crew – which establishes our millionaire as someone with time on their hands and a social conscience, or as a researcher for a documentary. Without exception the millionaire heroes and heroines of each show are shocked by what they discover and equally amazed by the levels of commitment of 'ordinary people' who have made things happen with incredibly slim financial resources.

Cut to the end of each programme, the millionaire reveals his true identity and hands over cheques to support the people and projects that have touched them the most. Even though some of the sums given are quite modest, they are always beyond the wildest expectations of the people who have befriended their new volunteer. An emotional and touching moment where people well up (on the screen and no doubt in living rooms throughout Britain) before our heroes return to their comfortable family life chastened, and vowing to be better people.

It is easy to be cynical about the programme and dismiss it as more cheap reality TV – which at one level of course it is. But some of the millionaires definitely 'get it.' Take Gary, an 'ordinary, hard-working, good bloke' who went under cover in Blackpool telling everyone that he had worked in a scrap yard all his life and wanted to turn his hand to some charity work. Gary didn't own up that he actually owned the scrap yard, which he'd built up from a £100 gift from his grandfather and which had made him a millionaire. Cut to Gary eating his breakfast in a café where he noticed a poster for Donna's Dream House.

It turns out that Barbara, who owns the café, also runs a hotel for terminally ill children named after her daughter, Donna, who died aged 21. Donna had always wanted to start a house for sick children so that they could have free holidays. Barbara and her husband, Len, had taken up the challenge in her memory. We visit the house, which operates as a free hotel for families to enjoy a seaside break, financed entirely from donations and fundraising efforts and run by volunteers, overseen by Barbara and Len. With no paid staff Donna's Dream House has already given a holiday to over four hundred sick children and their families.

At the end of the programme a genuinely amazed and moved Gary reveals his millionaire status and gives the disbelieving couple a cheque for £20,000 – cue hugs all round and the quiet remark from Barbara that a guardian angel must have been looking after them because things were beginning to get a bit tight. Gary turns out to be a gem. He not only gives money to Donna's Dream House, but returns to Blackpool with his fourteen-year-old son, who spends some of his summer holidays working there, and he also gives Barbara and Len another significant sum to extend the facilities of Donna's Dream House.

To its huge credit the format of Secret Millionaire makes sure that the focus is on small, grassroots initiatives; the local boxing club, gardening for children, visits to the elderly, a brass band and social club for old soldiers, food distribution for people who have absolutely nothing. Its researchers have uncovered hundreds of small organisations, throughout the UK, working in their own communities to make a difference, with people who are doing it for love more often than money, combining generosity and action on a daily basis, almost always with no official funding. Look carefully and you will see the true spirit of the nation.

The point of including it here is that it illustrates on the one hand how distanced the millionaires have become from the struggles of ordinary people, even when they return to the town they grew up in and reflect on their own modest childhoods. More importantly, it also highlights the astonishing numbers of so called 'ordinary people' who prop up our society, mostly unnoticed and unrewarded, working the most unimaginable hours and doling out help and love often at huge cost to themselves. To me they – not the millionaires – are the real heroes of the programme.

....

Talking 'bout a revolution

In other times, histories and cultures, inequalities of wealth such as those we see today, along with profligate extravagance in the face of poverty, have led to revolution: palaces sacked, the ruling elite executed or forced to flee their country.

The French revolution, with its call for 'Liberty, Equality and Fraternity'. The Russian revolution, aiming to establish an egalitarian, classless, stateless society based on common ownership. The American revolution, based on the declaration that 'all men are created equal, that they are endowed by their Creator with certain unalienable Rights, that among these are Life, Liberty and the pursuit of Happiness.'

Almost every country in the world has had a revolution at some stage in its history. Perhaps it's time we had one too.

THE JARROW MARCHERS

Even the traditionally polite folk who inhabit these isles and form orderly queues at bus stops have had a few attempts to rebel. In October 1936, 200 protesters led a march from the town of Jarrow to the Palace of Westminster in London, a distance of almost 300 miles (480 km), to protest against unemployment and extreme poverty.

The march was to find jobs to support Jarrow men and their families. It was also a bid for respect and recognition, not only for the people of Jarrow, but for others in a similar situation all over the country. The marchers had no resources other than their own determination, and some good boots supplied by the public. During the march, wherever the marchers stopped for the night, the local people gave them shelter and food. The marchers arrived in London on 31 October, almost a month after leaving. Perhaps they didn't achieve much – 12,000 signatures on a petition handed into Parliament; £1 each to get the train back from London. The ship industries remained closed. But they did carve themselves a place in history, a little respect, and the proof, through all those who fed and clothed and helped them on their journey, that this is a generous nation.

But we don't do revolutions. We protest. In my more radical moments, I have imagined a proud day when all the very poorest people in Britain, the most displaced and the homeless, single parents and the unemployed, people living in cities, towns and villages all over Britain, simply up sticks and head for London. Walk, as the Jarrow Marchers did, or hitch a lift, or get a bus, in a mass, quiet, non-violent protest, in the spirit of Gandhi and Martin Luther King Jr. For no other purpose than to remind those working in Government and the City that they exist, albeit hanging on to life by a thread. Simply to shame the Government, the politicians, those who work in the City and most of all the cruelly arrogant and stupid people who claim that there 'really are no poor people in Britain'.

They could draw up a simple protest petition, hand it in to Downing Street, and then quietly turn around and go home again. Along the way they would be fed and cheered by the people – that is you and I – who have food, warmth and decent incomes, and are occasionally given to moan between meals about house prices, schools, the deplorable state of British fashion and of course the EU and the euro.

Would this make us a more generous country and people? Perhaps, as, in interview after interview, individuals or groups explained the reality of their desperate lives in a country that couldn't look after them but could spend over £38 billion on defence spending each year, including £4.5billion on military operations in Afghanistan and Iraq. To introduce those countries to the benefits of democracy. The stories would touch us, shock us and, perhaps, make us want to do something about it.

The Post-Bureaucratic Age

There is one piece of good news on the horizon for community activists and local heroes; an end to bureaucracy. In an ideal world we could pay our taxes and trust the government to get on with it. The chancellor's budget would sort out the priorities, and the various departments would ensure that resources were allocated to the right pot. Another bevy of hardworking officials would invite a variety of organisations, including charities, to submit their tenders, with work plans, outputs and outcomes, staff levels, qualifications, diversity policies, environmental statements and more. But we all know that doesn't happen. Instead the dead hand of bureaucracy ensures that only a small proportion of our money ends up doing what we hoped it would: helping and supporting people. The rest goes in management, in procedures and best practice, in audits and accountability. This is no-one's fault: it is right that our money should be carefully spent, and in a vast bureaucratic machine management processes, supported by an audit trail in writing, are the only way to do that – with the media ready to pounce on any perceived slip-up.

Almost every political party, at every election, trumpets its intention to give power back to the people. What makes it much more relevant today is the power of the internet, and the life-changing access to information it brings. The hope is that this new transparency will encourage new individual and community initiatives. In future, data that has been held by the Government will be made available to all online, so that, for example, all Government contracts over £25,000 will be available for all to see. This will allow small, local businesses, which may be more efficient, to challenge and compete with existing contractors. Local crime maps, showing information previously held only by the police, will be put online, showing you which crimes have been committed in the streets near your home, or in the town where you live. Your energy bills will carry a visual comparison of your quarterly bill with the average bill in your area and the bill for the most energy saving home, allowing you to compare them with your own and perhaps save both money and energy. No more official nagging to turn your lights off.

It will impact on councils and public buildings too. In summer 2009, Windsor and Maidenhead Council began publishing real-time information on the internet about the energy consumption of their buildings, where local people could monitor it. As a result energy bills have fallen by fifteen percent. The mere knowledge that they were being watched was enough to get council workers to switch off unnecessary lighting and unused computers. In Australia, an app has been developed – 'It's Buggered, Mate' – to allow people to report faults directly to their local council, and find out what action has been taken.

At the heart of the concept of the Post Bureaucratic Age is the hope that public services begin to behave more like successful businesses, focussing on customer satisfaction and reacting rapidly to what the public actually want. The public will be able communicate directly and immediately with councils, hospitals and utility companies. The possibilities are limitless, but there's certainly hope here of more reactive, less inefficient public services in which community involvement is not just possible, but encouraged.

Take the first step

Here is a starter list of practical things that you could do to support your local community. You can no doubt think of many more. You absolutely don't need to be a millionaire. Remember that, taking your lead from the Food Chain, you can set up a group where everyone does a little, which adds up to a lot. Changing the remit of the book club to helping kids read for example. It may be the thought that counts, but it is the action that matters.

Search out a local cause. What you are interested in or feel passionate, even angry about. Education? Health? Disability? Homelessness? The Arts? Then search out the charities working in your local community, ask them what help they need and if they use volunteers. There are more small, grass roots organisations busily going about their work helping local people than you could possibly imagine, nearly all of which will welcome you with open arms. Do-it (**www.do-it.org.uk**) and Volunteering England (**www.volunteering.org.uk**) are a good place to start.

Sign up. Join your local Transition Towns organisation (see p.182), Friends of the Earth or other local group concerned with protecting your local environment. Or get a group together with a view to becoming a Transition Town.

Help out. If you are good with children or have kids at school locally, simply offer your services. If you plan to help regularly, be prepared to be CRB checked. Opportunities are likely to include mentoring, providing homework support, reading help, helping teachers supervise outings and breaks – or step back and offer your services as a member of the PTA or school governor.

Provide community transport. Lots of groups around the country ferry people who are elderly or disabled to clubs, hospital, friends, doctor, shops, library etc. There might be a local community bus service, but one of the reasons for being driven in a private car is that not only is it more flexible, but you can also have a decent conversation with someone who is housebound and a bit starved of company. As a volunteer you will be paid mileage.

Take someone shopping. I know you can do it online but
many elderly people don't have a computer and anyway
that's not the point. They appreciate being able to get
out, seeing what is available and maybe doing a little
impulse shopping. If you are pressed for time collect
their shopping list; if not be prepared to slow down, go
round with them and offer to read the labels. It is all too
easy to pick up the wrong canned beans, or even toma-
toes instead of beans, when your eyesight is not as good
as it was. And suggest things you think they might like
so you can steer them in the right direction.

Visit the hospital. Offer to take people to and from hospital
for their appointments. A friend of mine once volun-
teered to take a boy who had been hurt playing hockey
to hospital. She ferried him there, waited for him to be
treated then took him back to the school. She has continued to do school 'medical runs' for several years. Or
become a hospital visitor. Ring the local hospital, ask for
their visitors' group, and ask them who needs cheering
up.

Make a friend. Loneliness is a curse of our age. Think of having no family close by, coming back to an empty house
after a spell in hospital, not being able to get on the bus
to visit friends. A huge number of people are socially
isolated and many charities run befriending networks
that will try to match you up with someone who shares
your interests. My nephew, just 30, spends a couple of
hours an evening a week with a bachelor in his 80s. They
get on like a house on fire. A neighbour has committed
to mentoring a family going through a rough patch on a
regular basis for a year. She is volunteering with a local

charity that found that this sort of help keeps children out of the care system.

Cook a simple meal and ask someone you wouldn't normally socialise with to share it with you. We are not talking dinner parties and hard work. Quick, simple food – pasta and salad or soup and cheese is fine. It is the shared company, news and friendship that's most important. The very fact that you cared enough to ask them round.

Make a home visit. There will be someone you know who's unwell. Or finding life difficult. Or just alone. Make contact. If nothing else, ring, and listen rather than talk. If you've the time, arrange to visit. Taking flowers or a magazine is optional; it's your time that'll be valued.

Revamp that patch of waste ground. What might seem an unsightly, odd-shaped wasteland where people dump their rubbish has huge potential. Get a group together, clear it up and get planting – wild flowers, rambling roses, runner beans, potatoes; anything that will make people think twice before chucking an empty can on it. It's amazing how much satisfaction can be gained from a small space, it gives kids a chance to get muddy and turns an eyesore into something you can be proud of.

Join a committee. I've deliberately left this till last. It's not for everyone, but communities need school governors and local parish councillors. Don't wait to be asked; don't moan on any longer about the pothole that hasn't been filled. Find out who to contact and put your name forward.

8. Global poverty

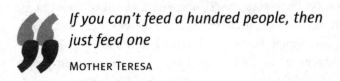

If you can't feed a hundred people, then just feed one

MOTHER TERESA

You have the power

Clark Kent is a slightly geeky, mild-mannered reporter for the Daily Planet newspaper. Under the cover of this very ordinary life he lives another, as the ultimate hero Superman, possessing extraordinary powers – "faster than a speeding bullet, more powerful than a locomotive, and able to leap tall buildings in a single bound". He has super-human strength, x-ray vision, super-hearing and the ability to run at amazing speeds, leap incredible distances and to fly.

He's been around since 1933, invented by Jerry Seigel and Joe Shuster, who were in turn inspired by heroes such as Samson and Hercules. The concept was to create a superhero who would right wrongs and fight for social justice and against tyranny.

'What is all this to do with me?' you ask. Perhaps Superman's enduring appeal has something to do with an aspiration to have a bit of Superman in ourselves. Let's assume for a moment that most of us have ordinary jobs that pay the bills and ask ourselves from time to time whether there is more to life. The message is, there is! We all have the ability to shed our ordinary lives, if only for a short while, put on our Superman outfits and do something that will right a few wrongs.

We can have much more fun and add meaning to life when we look for the superhero opportunities rather than wait for them to come to us. We all have the power to achieve extraordinary things, beyond the imagination of most people.

By 'most people' I am referring to the very poorest people in the world; the 'bottom billion' who live on the edge of life in extreme poverty, on less than $1.25 a day.

By contrast you already have super-human powers – the ability to fight for social justice and human rights and save lives. Today. And to paraphrase Mother Teresa, if you can't help a billion, that's no reason not to help just one.

Time to show up

Procrastination isn't excusable. It is time to show up in life, grab the opportunity and make a real difference. You can save the life of an African child by giving them food and medicine today. Tomorrow will be too late. International travellers protect themselves against malaria, but this is still the biggest killer in Africa; yet it can be prevented at minimal cost. You can provide education for an orphan or a street child so they have a chance to escape poverty, and lift generations of their family away from a life of hunger and disease. You can actively support and provide funds for organisations that fight for human rights – reducing sex trafficking, child labour, slavery and torture.

To the child saved, the orphan educated or the tortured prisoner released, you will quite simply be a hero. A real life Superman – or woman – using your own extraordinary powers; intelligence, money and even bloody-minded determination, to improve the lives of your fellow human beings.

We are all supposed to be global citizens, in the sense that we live in a truly interconnected world. Many of us have travelled to parts of the world that our parents could only dream about. A couple of webcams, an internet connection and Skype and it costs nothing to chat face-to-face for hours to someone on the other side of the world. Basic computers, with internet access and a screen that's readable in bright sunlight, are available for $199. Solar and wind technology is reducing dependence on non-existent electricity. And that's before the rise of the mobile phone, Facebook and Twitter generation – witness the immediate impact on news reporting during the Iranian elections in 2009: thousands of films available instantly on You Tube and Tweets by-passing government attempts to block them.

Ignorance is no longer an excuse. Our access to world news is 24/7 and anyone reading this has the resources to source information worldwide in seconds. Being informed we can choose to engage and help people in other parts of the world quickly and instantly if we want to. It is surprisingly simple to be generous and to spread generosity.

Before you say, 'Yes, but I don't have the time to check this all out', here are a few stats.

Live simply that others may simply live

The World Bank defines extreme poverty as not having enough income to meet the most basic human needs for food, water, shelter, clothing, sanitation, health care and education. It estimates the number of people living in extreme poverty (those with incomes of less than $1.25 per day, or around 85p), at 1.4 billion.

All those people, a shocking twenty percent of the world's population, face a daily struggle for enough food and water just to survive.

FAMINE – NOT JUST HUNGER
....

'We imagine that 'famine' is being hungry and thirsty, but when you go to a famine area you realise the complete nothingness and emptiness of famine – it is truly unimaginable. There is no reason to wake up, no reason to be up, nothing to do once you are up, no activity, no energy; nothing to sit on – everything has been sold – no animals; you just wake up and sometime later you go back to sleep. There is . . . absolutely . . . nothing, complete emptiness – soul and spirit drained.'

David Gold, Glimmer of Hope, in Ethiopia.
....

Thirty thousand people die each day of extreme poverty. That's a football stadium full every day, or the entire audience at the Hyde Park Live 8 famine concert, dead in eight or nine days. The Haiti earthquake every week. Someone's mother, father, daughter or son, about every three seconds. For a sobering reminder, go to the Make Poverty History website (www.

makepovertyhistory.org) and watch one of their short videos.

A minute is twenty-one deaths. The best way to grasp this, or rather to begin to get it, is to hold up your hands and click your fingers every three seconds. If you're a quick reader at least two hundred people will have died in the time it takes you to read this chapter.

By contrast, the World Health Organisation tells us that in the 'developed world' a billion people are overweight or obese, on diets and in gyms. As mentioned in chapter 4, half the food we buy is wasted between the plough and the plate. Thirty percent is thrown away. The amount of food thrown out each year in North America and Europe alone is enough to feed the world's hungriest people three times over.

It is incredibly easy to glaze over when people start reeling out numbers like these. But the fact remains that in an hour's time over a thousand people will have died of starvation, while a thousand people living near you overeat, or leave and throw away enough food to have fed them.

Those dying are in another country, out of sight and out of mind, while you are simply getting on with your busy, stressful life, trying to lose weight or get to the supermarket in time to buy a couple of microwaveable chicken curries before it closes.

Being obsessed with ourselves and our own needs whilst turning our backs on a billion of the poorest people on the planet is, simply, grotesque. While one part of the world's population gorge themselves into an early grave, an equal number starve to death.

If this is where 'survival of the fittest' takes us, we need to set off in another direction. To quote the cartoonist Bill Watterson, 'sometimes I think that the surest sign that intelligent life exists in other worlds is that no one has tried to contact us.'

Aliens living in their more advanced worlds and star systems presumably look at their version of Sky News in the evening, enter 'Earth' on their remote controls, and stare in disbelief at man's inhumanity to man.

It may be that future generations, too, will look back on this time and regard our behaviour as a crime against humanity, in much the same way as we now look back on slavery. It took William Wilberforce forty years to get parliament to abolish slavery. His fight was mostly against the commercial interests of the day, heavily reliant on slave labour. He gave his life to the Abolition of Slavery Bill, but success came at another price. The Bill was passed only when a sum equivalent to £20 million in today's values was paid to compensate landowners and businessmen. In the twenty-first century more than half of the world's largest economies are not countries but commercial enterprises. Perhaps our challenges are not so different.

IN ETHIOPIA, THIS WINTER

In Ethiopia, six million people face starvation this winter. These are a wonderful people with their own long cultural history, families – mothers, fathers, children – who once owned farms with cattle and lived simple, happy, fruitful lives.

And then the climate began changing. The rains failed not once but twice, and after their farms had failed to produce crops, their animals had been sold and they were unable to support their families' lives or their own, their world simply collapsed. These people are not ignorant or stupid, not reckless or spendthrift, not corrupt or work shy. They are quite simply in the wrong place at the wrong time.

It's all a waste of time

No doubt you can reel off a whole load of reasons why you have decided not to act. Like most people, you probably doubt that you can make any difference. And you justify this with the usual excuses: 'charity begins at home'; 'all overseas governments are corrupt'; 'most of the money goes on 4x4s, five-star hotels and administration'; 'the money never gets through to the people who really need it'.

But you are wrong. The people working in most aid agencies do outstanding work – think of those working in dangerous war torn areas like Darfur; or in drought-ridden countries like Ethiopia; or who reach the victims of earthquakes before their governments can respond, as in Haiti.

Some governments are corrupt, but this is not solely an African sport. Western democracies are heavily infiltrated and influenced by lobbying firms, and have their fair share of scandals, financial and political. Think Enron, or our very own recent parliamentary expenses scandal. Some aid is inefficient, but there are ways to give that ensure your money goes straight to where it is most needed. I have often observed that those with the most definite and unchallengeable views are those with the least knowledge, who have desire to learn more, much less go on a field trip to find out. They are just 'right'. Perhaps some of them simply want an excuse for not giving when they never actually had any intention of giving anyway.

Luckily, most of us are not like that. From Live8 to Children in Need, the Haitian earthquake to the 2004 tsunami, the British people have proved that they can be fabulously generous. The tsunami killed nearly 230,000 people in eleven countries and the British public donated £350 million to DEC (the Disasters Emergency Committee) and a further £50 million directly to the aid charities. We trusted them to get the money to where it was needed then. For Haiti, too, hundreds of millions have been raised. In these cases massive media coverage, peer pressure and sometimes the fact that we knew people who were involved, encouraged us all to give. This is great, but you don't have to wait for a disaster, or for Bono and Bob Geldof, to be generous.

The wrong sort of aid

In fairness to the gloom merchants, let's acknowledge that they do have a point. Not all aid is well-directed or appropriate, and disastrous mistakes have been made in the past.

Dambisa Moyo was raised in Lusaka, Zambia before a high profile career with Goldman Sachs and as a consultant to the World Bank. In her book Dead Aid she argues that 'aid has been, and continues to be, an unmitigated political, economic and humanitarian disaster for most parts of the developing world.' Moyo is pretty cynical about governments who take the cash which fuels corruption and interferes with the rule of law. Her views were echoed in a conversation I had with a highly respected, low-key, Indian philanthropist. 'You have to understand', he murmured gently, 'that there are two C's in India, caste and corruption. And, of course, the most sought after jobs in India are as a civil servant in a regional government. They get paid for doing their job, handing out money as directed by central government, and they get paid by the people they're handing the money out to. It's good for them, no? To be paid twice.'

Moyo argues her point from an economist's point of view, that lack of transparency discourages investment, so economic growth slows leading to fewer jobs and more poverty. Donors give more aid and the cycle starts all over again.

Michael Norton is more the practical, hands-on, type. He has founded several successful NGOs and written numerous books, the most interesting and entertaining of which is *365 Ways to Change the World* – how to make a better, fairer, freer, greener world every day (www.365ACT.com).

Michael has been proactively involved with Indian and African NGOs for many years. He is not a fan of aid agencies. In his view they become arrogant, treat people – even their donors – badly and turn into outcome machines, where the outcomes are promised but never really delivered.

Michael illustrated his point with a story about a visit to a village in Uganda with the head of a large, well-known overseas NGO. The boss was a well-meaning guy who spent most of his working hours in an office with a team of very bright and educated Africans, compiling reports for overseas donors. When they arrived at the village the head man presented them with a list of thirty-four things that they would like funded.

Michael asked for the list to be read out, one item at a time. After each request he asked three questions.

- Is this something you could do by yourself entirely?
- Do you need a little bit of help?
- Do you need a lot of help?

Of the thirty-four requests, twenty-seven were jobs the villagers either needed no help with at all or only a little, leaving seven where the NGO was really needed. Yet in ordinary circumstances the NGO would simply have approved the list, and ticked them off as successful 'outcomes'. It was a classic case of learned dependency.

'The development agencies' role is to empower communities,' Michael explained, 'yet this community was sitting there not doing anything. The development programmes weren't changing life much anyway, and what they wanted they could mostly do themselves. And if you learn to do the easy things yourselves, or with a little help, you're more able to cope with the more difficult ones later'.

We are the problem, not 'them'

What starts as a genuine desire to help gets lost at every stage. It's incredibly difficult for our Department for International Development (DfID) to work out what will work best at a micro level in a country with a different culture. In addition, governments deal with governments, and we know from our own experience that bureaucratic procedures are rarely effective, even before we take corruption into account. Non-governmental agencies should, and often do, perform better, but somewhere along the line we've left our instincts, and our common sense, behind.

If everything depends on outcomes and targets which have been agreed in advance in an office somewhere, quite often in a different country, people will say whatever their sponsors want to hear in order to get hold of the cash, and report back on successes whatever the actual outcome. Which leads to ever more stringent controls and an increasing cycle of reporting requirements, with almost as much energy put into trying to monitor the results, as into the aid in the first place.

For something to succeed it needs to be generated by the people, with the people and for the people. We need to listen. We need to trust them to get on with it. We need to stop being patronising and assuming we know best. I've come across too many stories of disillusioned gap-year travellers, who confirm tales of overseas aid workers living the life of Riley in former colonial outposts and of projects clustered round international airports for ease of access. The daftest story involved the donation of a reindeer from a Scandinavian charity to an Ethiopian village, at absurd cost and with a predictably unhappy outcome! More common are tales of abandoned wells, rusting vehicles and failed tree plantations, often for the simplest of reasons; lack of training, use of inappropriate materials, failure to provide or fund spare parts.

The right sort of aid

It doesn't need to be like this. And, in the main, it isn't. We have learnt from the past – sometimes even from the distant past, as when Oxfam took their incredibly successful campaign 'Give a man a fish and you feed him for a day; teach a man to fish and you feed him for a lifetime' from an ancient Chinese proverb. We're encouraged to give a chicken or a goat, with the potential for eggs, milk, biofuels and the whole village economy, not just a meal. Michael Norton is again worth paying attention to when he says that 'You can't do things **to** people. You can't really do things **for** people. For example teach a child who doesn't want to learn. People will only really change if they learn to help themselves. You can only do things **with** people. Working to encourage them to do things themselves.

The best aid agencies have learned how to do this. When there is trust they can ask open-ended questions and get honest answers. 'What do you most need?' – an open question, asked by someone who had worked a long time in the slums in Bangladesh of a woman there. The answer 'a private place for the women to shower'. Hardly a headline for a fundraising ad. Behind the answer, though, lay the knowledge that without it the women, all Muslim, were getting up at 3am (before the men were around) to wash at the public pump. It doesn't take long for the penny to drop about the impact of sleep deprivation on half the adult population of the slum and their ability to live a decent life and maintain their dignity. But it is not a priority I, personally, would have thought of.

THE REAL SLUMDOG MILLIONAIRES.

Millions of children really do live on the streets of India, work from the age of four upwards and, just as in Danny Boyle's film *Slumdog Millionaire*, rag-pick, beg for food, and clog up the traffic by doing gymnastics at the traffic lights for money. People working with these children say that many are street-wise well beyond their years, having spent their lives in a daily struggle to find enough food to survive and somewhere safe to sleep. Some are extremely motivated and do exceptionally well at school if one can only get them there.

I am sitting on the floor of a vocational training centre, run by an NGO in Jaipur, the 'pink city' in Rajasthan. Next to me, fourteen-year-old Tulsi is chatting happily and patiently explaining, between giggles, how she makes jewellery. The eldest of a family of five kids, her home was a temporary tent next to the main Jaipur–Agra highway on the outskirts of town (that's where most of them are, so they don't upset the tourists). When she was eight, both her parents died of TB and she became mother to her brother and three sisters, begging for food to survive. Unusually, the slum had fewer girls than boys so the traditional dowry system was reversed.

Tulsi's remaining relatives decided that she and her sisters would be married off and that they would pocket the dowries; a much older man offered to marry Tulsi. Child marriages are unlawful, but in rural Rajasthan, few care.

Luckily, this time, someone called the child helpline run by I-India, a charity that helps the street children of Jaipur and which is known and trusted by the slum community. A team from I-India arrived; the community wouldn't let the kids go. The police were called; the children were allowed to leave. And after a few days, when tempers had cooled, I-India was granted formal custody of Tulsi and her siblings. Today Tulsi is as bright as a button, speaks good English and lives in one of the charity's six children's homes, combining school with vocational training. She gets paid for her jewellery, has her own bank account and wants to become a social worker.

The founders of I-India are a remarkable couple. In the early Nineties, Prabhakar Goswami was an associate professor of sociology at an affiliated college of the University of Rajasthan; his wife, Abha, was a researcher for a large newspaper group. UNICEF and the state government approached them to conduct research into street children in Rajasthan and they undertook the project jointly. They were so moved by the children they met that they decided to shift from research into action.

Their own childhoods fuelled their passion and commitment: Prabhakar himself was brought up in a Jaipur slum, and Abha lost both her parents when she was young. One day, Abha simply packed some schoolbooks and toys onto a bicycle rickshaw and started visiting the children living by the road. Thus the School on Wheels began. It is now a small bus packed with teaching materials, a driver and two teachers, visiting sixteen slums and teaching and feeding 1,250 children a day.

On the day of our visit to one of the slum schools the children sat on the floor of the area outside the school and recited their maths tables with an enthusiasm and knowledge which would be impossible to find in a similar school in the UK.

The Shower on Wheels followed. A water lorry, which tours the same slums, provides the children with soap and toothpaste and hoses them down in a great noisy chaos. And an Ambulance on Wheels provides practical medical help and takes the more seriously ill to hospital. Then came six separate residential homes, three for boys and three for girls, and the vocational training centre, Ladli, where girls learn how to make jewellery and the boys are taught to make cards and bags: you can buy the products online at www.ladli.org.

They are paid at the end of each month. Many have their own bank accounts and save; some give the money to their hard-pressed parents. Every day, the charity helps three thousand street children. And incredibly, the whole programme only costs around £100,000 a year – that's about £33 a year per child.

••

Trust and Risk

Once, all development aid was based on the idea that poor people were not able to help themselves. Now, aid workers are having to learn how to listen and how to trust. The more you trust people, the more you get from them. Yes, it is not without risk, but risk is an integral part of life.

So, the challenge for many of us is to re-configure the way we think about a more sustainable global family. Listening requires generosity of thought. The leader of a major aid agency wisely remarked to me that poor people, from the slums of Delhi to the rural villages of Africa, don't introduce themselves as poor. They don't walk up to you and say: 'Hi, my name is Sanjay and I am poor'. They have their own real lives and dignity. We need to be prepared to respect the culture and values of an Ethiopian herdsman or an Amazonian hunter and accept that they have as much validity as our own. We, in the developed world, are not a super-intelligent race with all the answers.

It is only by listening that we come to understand and, over time, build trust. It is only by listening that we come to realise that there is no silver bullet that is going to change things overnight, or in a decade. Life is complex and societies in constant change. Communities are a bit like a delicate house of cards. With all the cards in place there is balance; remove one and the whole thing can collapse. We need to focus on hearing the messages we receive direct from the bottom billion, addressing the power imbalance, and recognising that our motivations may have previously been shaped by our media and vested commercial interests.

....

Go to the people,
Live with them, learn from them
Love them.
Start with what they know
Build with what they have.
But of the best leaders
When their job is done,
The task accomplished,
The people will say
'We have done it ourselves.'

Lao Tzu, sixth-century Chinese philosopher
....

We need to stop being patronising, assuming that our solutions are best. With access to the internet and a bit of time for research, any individual can find examples of aid that work, are proven and sustainable. We can find aid agencies that take the time to work on listening and empowering local, long-term change. And do something about it.

Micro credit for beginners

Microfinance hit the headlines in 2006, when the Nobel Peace Prize was jointly awarded to Mohammed Yunus and the Grameen Bank, which he founded.

The problem is that when you are poor you have no collateral, are deemed too high risk for established lenders and end up sucked dry by loan sharks. Yunus broke the mould when he set up Grameen in Bangladesh. He established a bank whose sole aim was to lend money to poor families, particularly women, and so help them set up their own small businesses. The loans are often tiny ($50 can be enough to get someone started) and always unsecured, but repayment is often understood as a communal responsibility. Village life is a community where groups gather to weave or sew to provide an income and no one wants to default. Grameen now has 7.95 million customers in 36 countries, 97% of whom are women. The repayment rate on the loans is a completely staggering 97.66%, a loan loss experience that is beyond the dreams of most western banks. They understand that people want to help themselves and can. And they take donations.

Barclays, RBS, et al eat your hearts out. It is nothing short of amazing that simply lending money to the poorest people on the planet gives them the opportunity to create their own small businesses, lift themselves out of poverty by their own efforts and repay the loans entirely. Microfinance organisations are now springing up all over the world. The model is proven.

In this internet age, anyone, in any country, can engage directly in microfinance. Kiva (www.kiva.org), for example, finds and works with locally based microfinance organisations, whose agents on the ground introduce budding village entrepreneurs. You can browse the entrepreneurs' profiles on Kiva, choose someone to lend to, and make a loan online. Though the donations are now pooled behind the scenes, you'll be helping someone make great strides towards economic independence and an improved life for themselves, their family, and their community. Throughout the course of the loan (usually 6-12 months), you can receive email journal updates and track repayments. Then, when you get your loan money back, you can lend it again to someone else.

On an even more local scale, Shivia (www.shivia.com) is a UK-based microfinance charity that works with communities living below the poverty line in India and Nepal. Shivia's donations really do reach the poorest of the poor, and the knock-on effect of their work is tremendous: families can eat properly and have access to health care; children can go to school; women have a voice and a sense of dignity. All this from loans which are typically just £120.

You'll have spotted it already, but the principle of microfinance is that it is small, personal and gets directly through to people at the grassroots. The sort of people who have previously had little education or knowledge of any banking system. Its impact is bottom up. And at the same time, it is a lending industry with a track record. Microfinance organisations monitor results, know what works and share that knowledge. However dubious you might have been about the power you have to change things for the world's bottom billion, this one definitely works.

MICROFINANCE IN ACTION

••

One of Shivia's loan recipients lives in a conflict-affected village in Western Nepal and lost everything in the civil war – her son, her husband and her dignity; she was raped. She spoke of how her life was one of doom and gloom three years ago but now "I have started my own business. I received training and learnt to read and write for the first time in my life. I have made friends through my group and I am now the President of my group! I have started a goat-raising business. I breed the goats and sell them. For the first time, I am able to eat three meals a day and my daughter is going to school. The loan has changed my life!"

••

Remittances

The largest source of incoming money to many developing countries is not from government aid or NGOs, but from remittances. The World Bank's 2005 estimate for remittances 'through formal channels' was around $167 billion and together with 'informal channels' (I wouldn't begin to know how you research that one) increased to more than $250 billion. It's not so surprising when you think about it: you know someone you want to help and send them cash. The vast majority, of course, comes from emigrants. Take my Zimbabwean friend; nearly every penny she manages to earn is sent back to relatives. Then think of the millions of Africans, Asians, Eastern Europeans and others who have left to find a better life abroad. Many people who have spent time working and volunteering overseas do the same; they meet people they believe in, know and trust, and they keep helping on their return. Millions of tiny, regular payments going in direct support to individuals and families. It may be for food, a school uniform, tuition fees, to buy land. It may not be spent on good things, but it will be spent locally, which is better than a commercial contract back to the west. Maybe you should send some too.

How one cappuccino can change the world

Small, local, direct. Generosity starts with knowing that we can trust people to help themselves. We know microfinance and remittances help. We know that aid agencies that listen find better solutions. Development is changing and our attitudes need to change as well, recognising that quality of life is not directly proportional to material comforts and that relatively low cost interventions can have amazing ripple effects. Another example from David Gold:

'We walked to the water well that is within the community and does not require the women to spend hours every day walking and queuing for water; usually carrying back-breaking pots. This well was hand-dug to a depth of fifteen to twenty metres and with the equipment had cost $2000. The well serves a community of approximately five hundred people. The simple calculation is stunning – $4.00 per person for life. For the price of a cappuccino, a human being gets access to clean water for the rest of their life.'

Clean drinking water is obviously a good thing. However, the power of water is incredible.

David listed the other benefits:

- less time to collect water and therefore the women spend more time in their community and on education, health and other community activities;
- school enrolment rate amongst younger women improves;
- sharp decrease in falls and accidents and illness;
- reduction in miscarriages;
- nutritional status improves as the women have more time to spend on food preparation;
- reduction in diarrhoeal diseases – sometimes by as much as 65%;
- overall improvement in healthcare;
- body and clothes are washed far more frequently, so there are fewer fleas and bugs that carry disease.

All of this is a 'forever', one-off, step-change that fundamentally improves peoples' lives – for not much more than the price of a bottle of Evian. It is not rocket science, nor hugely difficult to understand. It is just common sense. This is the true work of a superman or woman – any one of us – for just $4

It is surprisingly simple to help people in other cultures and countries. More than in any other period in human history we have the opportunity to act directly to give people less fortunate than ourselves the knowledge and practical assistance that they need to help themselves. We have the knowledge and the resources, practical and financial, to lift the bottom billion out of poverty. We simply need the will to do so.

BLESSED BRANCH

David Gold again, on making an unannounced and unplanned stop at an Ethiopian village, rather appropriately called Blessed Branch. The visitors entered on foot, vehicles parked out of sight.

'The village was clearly poor, with people living in mud huts. The villagers only had access to appalling water miles away, because the Italians had built a reservoir in the wrong place. People used the reservoir to wash their cars in, so the water was full of oil.'

'The villagers were living off goats' milk. I asked them what they did if they ever had surplus milk and have never forgotten their answer. 'We give it to poor people'. I was stunned: they 'give it to poor people' – they live almost entirely off goats' milk and, if they have a surplus, they don't take it to market, they give it to poor people!'

'We had a football with us, which we gave them, and the entire village and all of the people from a Glimmer of Hope were playing football together. They gave us everything. They played with us, and they partied with us, and they talked with us – and there was nothing in it for them. They didn't do it because they expected something from us – I was overwhelmed with their generosity.'

Take the first step

Keep an open mind. Recognise that the starving people whose pictures you see on the television news are not living on another planet, they are living on our planet. They are not 'entertainment', they are our people.

Millions of people living within a few miles of the EU. It is quite likely our actions that have indirectly caused the drought that made their crops fail and their cattle die. Recognise, too, that commercial interests lobby politicians and spend heavily on PR to feed the media. The scales are not balanced, especially in global markets.

Learn the facts. Motivate yourself to learn more about world poverty, and how you can be the change (check out some of the books in the Resources section). Listen to the small voices as well as the major change-makers. Discover grassroots projects by checking out The Funding Network (**www.thefundingnetwork.org.uk**) and Global Giving (**www.globalgiving.co.uk**).

Find out what works. It is more sensible to find out what's working than try to reinvent the wheel. That is what Grameen, Kiva and Shivia do. Sand dams that change the level of the water table for miles around, which in turn changes the local micro-climate. Biofuel projects – a few chickens or pigs provide manure, that becomes fuel for heat and electricity, which means evenings are lit after sunset so kids can do their homework. Eco toilets that can be built by local communities for as little as £20.

Spend less of your holiday on the beach. Travel broadens the mind, but less so in an international standard hotel with broken glass on top of the walls and security men on the gate. Many charities depend on overseas interest and encourage a visit in the hope of getting longer term support or selling products they produce. Build time in your holiday to visit and plan it ahead. Stay overnight if it's appropriate and possible. Include your kids. They're not only a great ice-breaker, the impact of seeing other kids with huge grins on their faces and joining in football games with bamboo woven balls will stay with them for ever. If you like what you see, take a risk, really listen to what they need and become Superman. Challenge your assumptions. Seeing kids showering in the open under hoses in a Kerala orphanage, our guide noticed my face. 'We set up the showers like this on purpose. It's what the kids are used to in the villages and most at ease with here.'

Be the change. If we put our minds to it we can all raise sufficient money to fund the salary of a teacher in a school in a developing country for a year – just a few hundred pounds. Four hundred can fund a water catchment tank in the Rajasthan desert. Or a thousand pounds will build a well. Search out first people who are trusted by the local community, who have listened, who know where the real priorities lie. Find projects operating at the grassroots – even if they are large. Stick with it. Have the satisfaction of seeing the change, which takes time. Dipping in and dipping out doesn't help a child who needs long term education or a village who can't fund a spare part for their well. Choose well and keep supporting. Learn from each other.

Twin your village with an African village, or your school with an Indian school or orphanage, or your town with an Asian town. For them the outside links and involvement with a source of Western money and expertise is often, literally, a lifesaver.

Help a Friend. Hugh's memory of being a VSO teacher for six months in his early twenties stayed with him. Twenty years later he returned to the village with his wife.

Instantly recognisable (English, over 6ft and blond) he was welcomed as a long lost friend. What hit him hardest was the obvious. His life had moved on, he'd built a career, he was on holiday in another part of the world. In the village nothing had changed. He returned, gave money, raised money, found the tax breaks and set up a school. Today, another twenty years on, it educates over a thousand children. And the village has changed. So find a friend who has a passion or commitment for a particular project overseas and support them. It is easier to support someone you know doing great work and even visit their project, than start your own NGO!

Engage with an aid agency. Don't wait for an emergency appeal. Find an aid agency which you admire and trust, or one that your friends and colleagues speak highly of. Engage, become a trustee, raise funds, share your expertise. We are all in this together.
www.aglimmerofhope.org

Become a microfinancier. Get involved with a small, personal and direct microfinance NGO like Shivia, or search Kiva for a selection of projects to co-fund.
www.shivia.com; www.kiva.org

9. The environment

We do not inherit the earth from our ancestors, we borrow it from our children

NATIVE AMERICAN PROVERB

Seeing is believing; climate change for beginners

Oxford, July 2009. Over six hundred people have gathered to take part in TEDGlobal, a conference whose mission is to share 'ideas worth spreading.' Over four days, TEDGlobal is hosting a series of eighteen-minute presentations on subjects and ideas as diverse as the way our brains work, taking sabbaticals, cities of the future and the future of the internet. The talks are given by seventy talented speakers from different countries and a wide variety of disciplines. They have come to share their knowledge and give an insight on their world. The audience listen, mix and mingle, eat together and exchange ideas at the excellent parties organised each evening. Business cards change hands at an astonishing rate, new friends and networks are formed – it is all hugely inspiring and informative; a week of 'brain food' and fun.

James Balog speaks on the last day. He is American – tall, lean and handsome in a healthy, outdoors sort of way – and a great communicator. He has eighteen minutes on the platform to talk to us about The Extreme Ice Survey which he set up, as a professional photographer, to help us understand the science of nature better. Balog and his team installed thirty-three time-lapse cameras, powered by the sun, in the Greenland Ice sheet, Alaska, the Rockies and Iceland. The cameras have been taking photos roughly every hour for almost three years. The resulting images allow us to see, and touch and hear and feel climate change in action. This is a 'seeing is believing' approach to make the invisible visible.

The cameras show, in compressed time, the true extent of the retreat of the ice cap and the melting of the glaciers. In Alaska the Columbia Glacier melts three kilometres between June 2006 and May 2009. We see what the camera sees. In Greenland, where temperatures are now 2.5 degrees Celsius warmer than in 1990, the Ilulissat Glacier is retreating at twice the rate it did twenty years ago: 125ft a day. In one sequence, ice that's a mile deep and three miles wide – 7.4 cubic kilometres in total – vanishes entirely in just seventy-five minutes. Balog understands that we find it difficult to visualise the dimensions so he illustrates his points. In those seventy-five minutes the ice equivalent of 3,000 Capitol Buildings in Washington, breaks up.

At the end of the presentation the audience is silent, then applauds. The melting of the ice over the last few years is quite clear for all to see. Everyone should watch it. In fact, why not pause and do that now? (www.ted.com/talks/james_balog_time_lapse_proof_of_extreme_ice_loss.html)

It's the way you tell 'em

I have come to the conclusion that the most serious problem facing the environment is communication. Or rather the lack of it. We are very bad at explaining it to ourselves. For us to pay attention, communication needs to be relevant, important and consistent. Ice-caps? We don't have those in the UK. The complexity of the inter-related issues making up the climate change and environmental debate, and the myriad of scientists, politicians and journalists banging on about it, don't help. Communication is everything.

The Green Alliance published a booklet in 2010 focusing on precisely these issues. Who trusts politicians and journalists? Scientists are notoriously difficult to understand. Add in a dose of mischievous publicity given to anyone who claims that it is all made up or cyclical and the intense lobbying of huge business corporations – eighty percent of all the world's food comes through just five international conglomerates – and you have misinformation on an almost criminal scale. All of which plays to our extremely strong desire to carry on our consumption-driven lives as normal and create a new global version of nimbyism – not so much Not in My Back Yard as Not In My Lifetime.

We are like the mythical frog being gently warmed in a pan of water. It is more comfortable in the water than out which leads, inevitably, to a dead frog. The concept that whole cities and countries could be underwater by the end of this century is simply not today's main meal. Passionate people talk about tigers and polar bears. We understand, but they're still in our zoos. The Rainforest is not the New Forest. If that was being scythed down on a daily basis with the residents being forced to move and the birdlife, badgers, foxes, rabbits and ponies dying, there would be mass protests.

Or perhaps, and this is a sobering thought, there would be no protests at all, the few who did complain would be written off as a group of self-serving nutters, and we would allow it to happen. The rainforest is so 'over there' it is extremely hard to get serious about it.

THE RIVET POPPER HYPOTHESIS

Stanford biologist Paul Ehrlich understands the communication issue and has created The Rivet Popper Hypothesis to make his point. In it he compares ecosystems to aircraft wings, held together by rivets.

'As you walk from the terminal to your plane, you notice a man on a ladder busily prying rivets out of its wing. Somewhat concerned, you saunter over to the rivet popper and ask him just what the hell he's doing.'

'"I work for the airline – Growthmania Intercontinental," the man informs you, "and the airline has discovered that it can sell these rivets for two dollars apiece."'

'"But how do you know you won't fatally weaken the wing doing that?" you inquire.'

'"Don't worry," he assures you. "I'm certain the manufacturer made this plane much stronger than it needs to be, so no harm's done. Besides, I've taken lots of rivets from this wing and it hasn't fallen off yet. Growthmania Airlines needs the money; if we didn't pop the rivets, Growthmania wouldn't be able to continue expanding. And I need the commission they pay me – fifty cents a rivet!"'

'"You must be out of your mind!"'

'"I told you not to worry; I know what I'm doing. As a matter of fact, I'm going to fly on this flight also, so you can see there's absolutely nothing to be concerned about."'

Erhlich goes on . . .

'Any sane person would, of course, go back into the terminal, report the gibbering idiot and Growthmania Airlines to the airline regulators, and make reservations with another carrier.'

'Rivet-popping on Spaceship Earth consists of aiding and abetting the extermination of species and populations of non-human organisms. Some of these species supply or could supply important direct benefits to humanity, and all of them are involved in providing – currently for free – public services without which society could not persist.

'Ecosystems, like well-made airplanes, tend to have redundant subsystems and other 'design' features that permit them to continue functioning after absorbing a certain amount of abuse. A dozen rivets, or a dozen species, might never be missed. On the other hand, a thirteenth rivet popped from a wing flap, or the extinction of a key species involved in the cycling of nitrogen, could lead to a serious accident. . . .'

....

We still have a chance to stop taking out the rivets. It will happen when we hear it from people we know and respect, when the word is on the streets and in the pub. When our politicians realise that we, the electorate, are serious about something being done and one hundred percent behind them doing it. So it is up to you and me. Think of it as insurance. Even if the odds are stacked against my house going up in flames, I'll insure it just in case. It doesn't cost that much to insure, but if I don't and the house burns down, there's no way I could afford another.

Even if I don't totally understand the global warming and ecological arguments, and don't feel the end of the world scenario will have any impact on me during my lifetime, it seems totally sensible to take out a bit of insurance on behalf of my younger relatives rather than stay with my head in the sand.

Climate change: myth or reality?

Despite recent reports of covered-up emails, errors in scientific research and more, the overwhelming evidence points to accelerating man-made climate change. As Tony Juniper, environmental adviser and former director of Friends of the Earth, has written 'Although there is still a rump of denial about the reality of human-induced climate change, the debate has moved on in recent years towards what we do about the problem, rather than whether we have one.' But even if you're not sure, it makes sense to act. I asked a thoughtful and well-informed friend of mine what he felt about climate change and the threat to the environment and his take on it all was instructive:

'I am inclined to believe the science which says that man is the chief cause of global warming. At the same time, I accept it is possible to explain the changes as part of a cycle which man has not caused. But I am convinced we should take remedial action as soon as possible because:

- of the precautionary principle. If the current predictions are correct, we should do something about it immediately. If we even suspect that they might be correct we should take action immediately in much the same way as we would all normally take out insurance against a possible risk. It is a sensible precaution.

- the measures being suggested will improve the quality of life for all mankind, even if the explanation for climate change turns out to be cyclical; both directly – cleaner air, saved rainforests and less-polluted seas – and through beneficial technological spin-offs created to conserve and harness renewable energy.

- buying less stuff encourages everyone to review what they actually need for themselves and their family – much less than we have been led to believe. A lot of our spending has morphed from 'I would like to have it' to ' I need it' without really thinking it through. The three R's are common-sense principles that everyone understands – Reduce, Re-use and Recycle

- there is a positive spiritual dimension. The west will have to make a proportionately greater sacrifice in relative living standards, which is an important step towards a more equitable and generous sharing of resources in the world. Live simply that others may simply live.

- the economic cost of acting now will be much less than acting later.

- finally, acting together as a global community towards a common goal will give fresh impetus to the spirit of international cooperation.

Environment, economy and population

It is not just the climate, it is the whole of our environment that is at risk. We have been brought up to acquire things on an unbelievable scale, all of which are manufactured or made using trees, crops and food growing on the earth or minerals from within it. Absolutely everything you and I live on comes out of the ground, is grown on it or feeds off it. We are part of this system, not apart from it, and we are dependent on it, not in control. Look around the room you are in: wood in chairs, floors and beams; cotton and wool in curtains, upholstery, clothing;

clay in crockery and bricks; metal in radiators, electrics and the building's structure; stone in floors, concrete and cement; silicone for glass; oil for paint, plastics, artificial fibres and to power the light and heat. Then take a moment to think about all of us living here.

Take food for example. As Carolyn Steel wrote in her book *Hungry City* 'Feeding cities arguably has a greater social and physical impact on us and our planet than anything else we do. Yet few of us in the West are conscious of the process. Food arrives on our plates as if by magic, and we rarely stop to wonder how it might have got there.'

'But when you think that every day for a city the size of London, enough food for thirty million meals must be produced, imported, sold, cooked, eaten and disposed of again, and that something similar must happen every day for every city on earth, it is remarkable that those of us living in cities get to eat at all.'

The United Nations forecasts a world population of 9.2 billion by 2050. That is almost fifty percent up on the current 2010 figure of 6.5 billion. Pause and add forty years to your own age, your children's age or, if you are feeling brave, your grandchildren's age. When they are still around, there'll be one and a half times as many people to feed, clothe, house and sustain as there are now. Given that a billion of the six billion in today's world already struggle to find the food, water and basic healthcare to live a decent life, what hope is there for the 2.7 billion who are about to join them? How on earth (sorry) are we going to feed all these people, to say nothing of finding them homes, clean water and a life worth living? It is going to be a huge challenge.

Governments stress the need to focus on economic growth. Businesses argue about the costs of environmental requirements. But if there's no environment, bye, bye business.

Economy and ecology aren't issues we can choose between. There's a clue in the Greek 'ecos' which means home or household. Ecology is the study of the home which is common to all of us: our planet. Economy is about managing the systems that make the planet function well and productively. This includes, but is not limited to, what we know today as economics. The disciplines are inseparable.

The United Nations Environment Programme (UNEP) got 1,400 scientists to contribute to a report, which took five years to prepare, called the Global Environment Outlook. They agreed that 'human consumption has far outstripped available resources. Each person on Earth now requires a third more land to supply his or her needs than the planet can supply.' No wonder the planet is stressed.

Biologist Paul Ehrlich again: 'as nature is progressively impoverished, its ability to provide a moderate climate, cleanse air and water, recycle wastes, protect crop from pests, replenish soils and so on will be increasingly degraded. The human population will be growing as the capacity of Earth to support people is shrinking . . . the familiar world of today will disappear within the life span of many people now alive.'

PALM OIL: SCOURGE OF THE RAINFOREST
....

Palm oil is vegetable oil. Though not listed in the ingredients as palm oil, it is a confirmed or suspected 'invisible' ingredient in 43 out of 100 of the UK's best selling grocery brands. Look closer and it's really 43 out of 62, since the hundred best selling brands include drinks. So what?

Palm oil is popular with manufacturers as it is the cheapest edible oil they can get. To source it, vast tracts of the indigenous forests of Indonesia and Malaysia have given way to palm oil plantations, a process that involves the loss of ninety percent of the wildlife in those areas. That means the indigenous population cannot hunt, so human life disappears from the area as well. In order to have soaps and detergents, chocolate, biscuits, snacks, bread and cereals we have jointly been responsible for wiping out an area equivalent to twenty-eight million acres so far in Indonesia alone. It is an interesting thought that as you munch through your breakfast cereal each morning you could be munching through a little portion of the rainforest and voting for the extinction of the orangutan.

However much we love Kit Kat, Dairy Milk, Special K, Pringles and Persil, they are not worth it until they stop using palm oil and shift to sustainable vegetable oil. The more you eat of and use this stuff, the more rainforest will have to be destroyed to grow more palm oil crops.

....

Rainforests, wildlife and the environment

The Amazonian Rainforest, the largest surviving on earth, spreads over a billion acres of Brazil, Venezuela, Columbia, Ecuador and Peru. Some people have called rainforests the 'lungs of the world'. They cover seven percent of the world's surface and provide twenty percent of the world's oxygen needs by continuously recycling carbon dioxide into oxygen. Free, gratis and for nothing. Just to make sure we are on the same page – oxygen is the stuff we need to breathe. More than half of the world's plants, animals and insects live in the tropical rainforests. They support the livelihoods of 1.6 billion people including many indigenous tribes with unique and irreplaceable cultures. They store water, regulate rainfall and are home to thousands of medicinal plants. They act as a natural climate regulator and global cooling mechanism. They absorb, store and recycle between ten and fifteen percent of our global carbon emissions just by being there.

Clouds created by the rainforest put twenty billion tons of water into the atmosphere, which falls as rain locally and thousands of miles away. The rain feeds rivers and lakes and supports millions of people whose lives depend on it for their own needs as well as food and crops. Reduced crops will, if you follow this through logically, impact commodity prices and the price of our groceries in the UK.

The forest is disappearing for a whole variety of reasons, but the over-arching impetus is economic. The insatiable demand for soybean, palm oil, logged wood, beef cattle and cereals generates cash. So an area the size of a football pitch disappears every four seconds. Short term gain is exchanged for longer term loss. In creating demand for the goods, we are effectively destroying the system that enabled their creation.

A more generous approach would be for every one of us to recognize our responsibilities for the stewardship of this wonderful and unique environment, with its ancient cultures and treasure trove of wildlife and plants. To agree that we need the rainforest much, much more than we need any more stuff.

It is estimated that between thirty-six and one hundred and fifty different species are becoming extinct every day. At the conservative end of the scale that's over thirteen thousand every year, mainly through deforestation. An awful lot of rivets. It is difficult to be more precise because biologists reckon many of the species have not yet been discovered, but if reality is at the top end of the estimate, we are destroying almost 56,000 species every year.

● ●

Tiger, tiger burning bright,
In the forests of the night,
What immortal hand or eye,
Could frame thy fearful symmetry?

William Blake 1757 - 1827

● ●

In the last hundred years ninety-five percent of the world's
tigers have disappeared as a result of hunting, poaching and
removal of their natural habitat. Bye, bye tiger. Such a shame
there won't be any anymore.

We are destroying the oceans too. Fish, with or without
chips, could soon be a memory. We will have eaten them all.
The bluefin tuna is now officially an endangered species, yet
is still being ruthlessly hunted down to supply our dining
tables and restaurants. It is already one of the most expensive
foods in the world and in Japan, where it is a delicacy, they
are stock-piling deep-frozen bluefin in anticipation of rising
prices come the inevitable global shortage.

Copenhagen: governments won't act

Fifteen thousand delegates and five thousand journalists
from 193 countries gathered in Copenhagen in December
2009 to try to hammer out a deal on climate change and save
our environment. In the end, in what one of my environmental colleagues described as a 'train wreck', the compromise
cobbled together was feeble, after an untold number of cha-
otic meetings and some very determined opposition from
several countries powerfully protecting their own sovereign
interests.

I doubt a decent result was ever possible. In most cases countries spoke in the same terms as they had done for years, directly to their national audiences. The agreement reached was pretty much the worst case scenario: no deal done on legally binding targets, no timetable and no independent monitoring system. The Chinese President remained in a room on his own summoning key leaders to see him individually, while sending his deputy to negotiate with other heads of state. In effect the Chinese were announcing their place in a new world order. With a large percentage of their population living in poverty, they need a growing economy and cheap supplies of energy (read coal) to prevent civil unrest and remain in power.

The American position was similarly pragmatic. America is in deep recession and in debt to the Chinese. Their priority was to defend their economy and get it growing again. In any case the chances of a climate change bill being passed by the Senate were very remote.

As Copenhagen descended into political chaos, people began to get the hint. Huge and unwieldy world conferences will always be derailed by political and commercial self interest and reality. The suspicion remains that even if 193 countries did agree to limit carbon emissions and to report on their progress each year, many would simply not do so.

As George Monbiot, the environmental journalist, wrote after the conference: 'goodbye Africa, goodbye south Asia, goodbye glaciers and sea ice, coral reefs and rainforest. It was nice to know you. Not that we really cared. The governments which moved so swiftly to save the banks, have bickered and filibustered while the biosphere burns.'

MONEY CANNOT BE EATEN

Only when the last river dries up
when the last tree is torn down
when the last animal is killed
only then will you understand that money cannot be eaten

Creek Prophecy

So it is down to us

We probably have ten to fifteen years to take steps to head off the levels of climate change that civilization will find near impossible to adapt to.

Politicians need our votes and businesses need our money. Starved of both, a change in mood can be forced. In the UK we are very fortunate, firstly because we have excellent campaigning organisations like Friends of the Earth and Greenpeace. Second because our major supermarkets are 'to the moment' efficient and responsive to public feedback and views. They know on the hour what is or is not selling, to whom and where. A downturn in sales of a particular product hits their tills, and therefore their profits, instantly.

We now each have a simple and straightforward choice as individuals. We can ignore the science, plough on and ignore what Al Gore famously called the Inconvenient Truth, blame China, India, America and join the twenty-first century version of the flat earth society. Or we can change our behaviour. We can engage, get a grip and learn more about the future of our planet and how to save it. And to those who argue that there's no point in us doing anything when the Chinese far outnumber us and might not be onside yet, how can we possibly expect them to change their ways if we set no example to follow? Mountains of reading and many expert witnesses later I, for one, am convinced that we need to act. But also that it is not yet too late to be generous and put the survival of future generations (for make no mistake, that is what's at stake) at the heart of our own actions.

What we can do

It is one thing to be a responsible citizen, buy low energy light bulbs and turn off the lights when we are not in the room; turn off our TVs at the plug, insulate our lofts, buy smaller cars or take the train rather than the plane. By doing all these things we save energy and, usually, money. A sort of environmental win/win situation – we are good and we get rewarded.

It is another and much more important thing to live responsibly and take action to save the planet for our children, our grandchildren and for future generations we will never know. This is more generous behaviour. We have to give of ourselves and change our habits. Stretch out from our comfort zone, stop living in a way that prioritises convenience, and choose to live our lives in a way that is responsible and respectful of other people, animals and the planet.

This takes us in the opposite direction from much that we take for granted. We are consumers, we have been told to believe in growing GDP and a rising standard of living. And that includes the freedom to travel, to chuck away products that are out of date or out of fashion, and to eat food out of season.

The way we spend our money places excessive and unnecessary strain on the ecosystems on which we depend to survive.

How far we drive determines how much petrol we use. Ditto how much we use our heating determines the amount of energy we use. When you buy baby veg from Africa, think not only of the freight costs but also the carbon footprint. In Felicity Lawrence's truly scary book about food production, *Not on the Label*, she tracks Kenyan beans as they travel over 4,000 miles to get to a UK supermarket shelf! Her plea is quite straightforward. Buy local, buy seasonal and support your independent retailers.

It is great to enthusiastically support campaigning charities like Friends of the Earth, Greenpeace or WWF. Or to buy Fair Trade goods – there are now over 3000 certified products, from coffee to chocolate, fresh fruit to T-shirts, with many of us prepared to pay a bit of a premium to improve the lives of the people who make them. Generous behaviour. However, it is the intangible things we do that can have an even greater impact.

The first and most important thing you can do is to learn more about what's happening. Engage with the issues and start talking them through with friends and neighbours. There is a very good chance that you and they will be shocked and staggered by what we are doing to our world, to the extent that you will wish to change some of the things you perhaps take for granted today. If there is one thing that companies, businesses and politicians really understand, and react to swiftly, it is a reduction or loss in income and support. Public opinion creates political action and change. If you stop buying unsustainable tuna the Japanese may not stop fishing for it straight away, but if thousands stop buying, there will be no market and less reason to fish.

A couple of years ago I asked two engaged environmentalists what it would take to get the message of climate change through to the people who govern our country. They both said the same thing. The way we use our votes and the way we spend our money.

Politicians of every colour only really understand a subject when the people they govern talk to them about it, in small groups and then en masse. And if there is one sure way to get a company's attention, it is to stop spending money with them. Our retailers and supermarkets have by far the best marketing antennae in the western world. They know what is selling hour by hour and forecast what is likely to sell by studying every variable from the political outlook to weather patterns. They will notice.

To make it simple, here are a few initiatives that communicate effectively and are keen to get you involved.

∙∙

'If you think you are too small to make an impact, try going to bed with a mosquito!'

The Dalai Lama
∙∙

Cool Earth

Cool Earth (www.coolearth.org) raise money to buy strategically placed areas of rainforest that would otherwise be sold to loggers and ranchers, so they can protect them from being cut down. They focus on rainforest that is in imminent danger and which, without intervention, would be cleared. The parcels of forest bought often form a protective blockade for tens of thousands of acres of adjacent forest. Through community rangers and satellite imagery they monitor the acquired land round the clock. They also put money in a local trust and make the local communities legal custodians of this land, enabling them to earn a better income through sustainable employment programmes. By supporting schools, clinics and sustainable jobs, Cool Earth makes sure forest protection goes hand in hand with better lives. They have made it incredibly simple for you or me to buy a tree or an acre, and thanks to supporters have protected 127,000 acres of rainforest so far.

10:10

Franny Armstrong doesn't take no for an answer! Still in her thirties, she has directed three high-profile documentaries, most recently persuading 620 people to 'crowd fund' the £820,000 she needed to produce 'The Age of Stupid'. In the film, actor Pete Postlethwaite plays the part of a man living alone on a devastated planet in 2055 asking: 'why didn't we stop climate change when we had the chance?' To Franny climate change is the great cause for her generation.

'I was born in the early Seventies, part of an MTV generation who were told by a million advertisements that the point of our existence was to shop more. Daunting though the task ahead may be, I feel enormously inspired and quite relieved that it turns out that we have something important to do. The people who came before us didn't know about climate change and the ones who come after us will be powerless to stop it.'

'So it's down to us. Other generations came together to overturn slavery or end apartheid or win the vote for women. There is nothing intrinsically more useless about our generation and there is no doubt what we have to do. The only question is whether or not we give it a go.'

10:10 (www.1010uk.org) is the action plan built on the foundations of 'The Age of Stupid'. It aims to get every sector of British society to reduce carbon emissions by 10% in 2010 – an achievable, immediate goal. 10:10's CEO Eugenie Harvey isn't daunted. She has already helped create 'We Are What We Do' and 'Change the World for a Fiver'. Even if you've never heard of 'We Are What We Do' (www.wearewhatwedo.org) you'll be aware of one of its legacies. The original cotton 'I'm Not a Plastic Bag' designed by Anya Hindmarch was their campaign, and helped inspire a 40% drop in the number of plastic bags used by supermarkets.

As the 10:10 website says, 'It's simple. You, me, that bloke walking his dog outside, your work, your kids' school, the council, the church, the chip shop. This campaign is for everyone.' As I write, 10:10 have signed up the new coalition government – 10:10 storms No. 10 – plus 60,000 individuals, over 2,000 businesses, more than 1,000 schools and colleges, The Sun, The Guardian, Stoke-on-Trent and Spurs football club. With practically no money and a huge amount of energy, 10:10 is succeeding in doing what so many have signally failed to do, making the challenges facing the environment understandable and getting people involved.

The End of the Line

One day we will ask, 'where have all the fish gone?' The answer will be, 'we have eaten them.' The End of the Line (www.endoftheline.com) is a film linked to a campaign to preserve global fish stocks. In 2000 the environmental journalist, Charles Clover, walked into the wrong briefing room in Brussels and discovered he was listening to a briefing on 'bottom trawling'. Horrified by what he heard he began to investigate what was going on and published the results in his book, *The End of the Line*.

The issue, again, is simple. We are fishing to extinction. 'Bottom trawling' is one element of this. It involves fishing fleets with sophisticated tracking devices using huge nets to trawl the sea bed, vacuuming up everything in their path: fish, coral, whatever. This is fishing on a huge, industrial scale. Each net could fit thirteen Boeing 747s across its mouth.

In 2006 film-makers George Duffield and Rupert Murray discovered Charles' book and negotiated the film rights. Their vision was to use the film to campaign for more sustainable fishing. They talked to organisations such as Greenpeace, WWF and the Marine Conservation Society, gaining support and tapping into their campaigning expertise and funding contacts. On release, simultaneously across 65 UK cinemas in 2009, it made an immediate impact. Cue Clover, Duffield and Murray knocking on the doors of politicians, civil servants and commercial interests to find that hardly anyone had thought about the problems of over-fishing and most were totally ignorant of the indisputable facts, namely: there is a finite number of fish in the sea, and over-fishing means that number is falling rapidly; without corrective action, we are in danger of seeing our entire global fish stock collapse within forty years.

Response from supermarkets was immediate. Waitrose, a partner in the development phase, implemented a very advanced sourcing policy for sustainably caught fish: after the film's release their fish sales grew by over fifteen percent. Both Asda and M&S followed suit. Prêt a Manger screened the film to their managers and now only buy sustainably caught fish.

This campaign isn't asking us to give up eating fish, but to eat fish sustainably caught so it's still there to eat forty years on. The End of the Line campaign is now focusing on helping to increase the area of the world's oceans protected in marine reserves, from 1% to 10%. There's nothing to stop Britain leading the world through creating sustainable fish policies. All we need is the political action to reinforce what people are already beginning to do.

No Net Loss

The concept of No Net Loss has been around for some time. It works like this. If I clear a forest, drain some wetlands, clear a construction site or mine for minerals, I do my best to avoid doing harm to the extent that I can, but when, inevitably, I cause damage to the ecosystem, then I agree to do something that will compensate for it. Generosity to the environment if you like: no damage or, in an ideal world, a net positive impact. Where I take something away, I enable it to be recreated elsewhere.

For climate change, No Net Loss means avoiding energy use altogether wherever possible, using energy as efficiently as practical, and offsetting the climate impacts of the energy used.

For biodiversity, it means pushing oil and gas, mining, utility, forestry, agriculture and tourism companies to adopt no net loss/net positive impact policies. Some leading global conglomerates have already done so and the pressure is growing.

The next step is to bring the concept of No Net Loss into our everyday lives through No Net Loss labeling. Together with sustainable sourcing and Fair Trade, we will be able to incorporate a No Net Loss kite mark. The manufacturer will guarantee that all components are from sustainable sources. There will be an audit trail to ensure environmental damage is minimized and the residual harm compensated for, and communities enhanced rather than destroyed in the process. We will be able to go to the supermarket and buy No Net Loss or Net Gain tuna, coffee or bread, and then choose No Net Loss jeans, computers, mobile phones and more in the High Street.

Even before this happens, we can all take part in the process today. We need to check where the products we buy come from and, for example, whether a particular brand of biscuit includes cheap but globally ruinous palm oil. If the answer is 'yes', stop buying it. If the answer is 'no' tell your friends, blog it, tweet it, spread the word. Nothing is as contagious as word of mouth and manufacturers and retailers are hugely sensitive to falling sales and emerging trends.

Transition Towns

'We truly don't know if this will work. Transition is a social experiment on a massive scale.' This unusually self-deprecating quote from the Transition Towns website (www.transitionnetwork.org) hides a very contagious movement. A Transition Town is a community set up to tackle the twin challenges of peak oil and climate change. The idea originated in Kinsale, Southern Ireland, took root in Totnes, Devon and has so far 'planted' 275 communities across the world. All have their own tailor-made action plans to reduce energy use and become more self reliant.

The purpose is to raise awareness of sustainable living and decrease the impacts of climate change. Transition communities start with a group of people who are concerned about their community, action-orientated and recognize the importance of a switch from a high-carbon, fossil-fuel-addicted way of life. People who live and work in their communities and therefore have local knowledge and are generous enough to develop long term solutions. Each person involved finds a passion – food, energy, business, currency, the psychology of change, even art – and forms a group to find local solutions to local issues.

Communities are encouraged to seek out methods for reducing energy usage and increase their own self reliance – a slogan of the movement is 'Food feet, not food miles'! Initiatives have included creating community gardens to grow food; business waste exchange, which seeks to match the waste of one industry with another industry that uses this waste; and even simply repairing old items rather than throwing them away. Totnes introduced its own local currency, the Totnes pound, redeemable in local shops and businesses to help reduce food miles while supporting local firms; an idea followed by many others including Lewes in Sussex and Whitstable in Kent.

Because every community is different, in ethnic mix, age range and social background, numerous different solutions are created.

Ben Brangwyn set up Transition networks to inspire and encourage a more interdependent way of life. For Ben the heart of Transition Towns is the need to build awareness around how ecology and our environment can work together to improve a local community. Part of the underlying philosophy runs as follows: if we wait for the governments, it will be too little, too late; if we act as individuals, it will be too little; but if we act as communities, it might just be enough, just in time.

Take the first step

These are a few things you can do to improve the environment, save money and live a happier, simpler life – with thanks to the 10:10 team. If you only manage a couple you could still end up healthier (from walking and cycling), with new friends (from swapping stuff and car-pooling), better off, having saved a big chunk of cash, and happy in the knowledge that you're part of a global effort to prevent castastrophic climate change.

Become properly informed. Follow the adventures and campaigns of environment organisations like Friends of the Earth (**www.foe.co.uk**), Greenpeace (**www.greenpeace.org.uk**) and the World Wildlife Fund (**www.wwf.org.uk**).

Do no harm; institute a personal 'no net loss' programme. If we all made a conscious effort to avoid companies and products that harmed our environment purely for the pursuit of profit, we would be taking a stand.

Ask where it comes from. Where does the food you eat come from, miles away or closer to home? From sustainable sources and suppliers, from Fair Trade projects, or are you helping to destroy the rainforest and wipe out indigenous people?

Fly less, holiday more. Swap plane for train, holiday nearer to home and take fewer but longer trips – same tanning time, dramatically less climate change emissions. Give up flying, or if you are going long-haul try to reduce your travelling to one return flight a year. Flying is bad news for the environment and the commercial lobby for more airports destroys homes.

Save 10%. Sign up to 10:10 and cut your carbon emissions and your energy costs by 10% in 2010; for tips and suggestions, check out the Energy Saving Trust (www.energysavingtrust.org.uk). Turn down your thermostat, turn off radiators in hallways and wear more jumpers all round. Then apply for a grant to insulate your loft and walls. Save big cash by changing light bulbs, replacing old fridges and freezers and always turning stuff off. Use your bill to see whether you cut 10% in 2010. **www.1010.uk.org**

Drive less. Leave your car at home one day a week. Walk, cycle or take public transport. Good for the heart, mind and body! Join a car-club rather than owning your own and share your ride to work with a colleague or two. If you are changing your car, buy a smaller one or a hybrid.

Eat better. Local, in-season fruit and veg produce the least emissions – and the less processed the better.

Have a meat-free day each week. Or even two. Which does more harm to the environment? An aeroplane flying round the world, or a cow munching grass? It's the cow. Or at least livestock generally, responsible for as much as 18 percent of greenhouse gas emissions, a higher share than transport. Livestock production also accounts for 70 percent of all agricultural land and 30 percent of the land surface of the planet. And that's before we get on to factory farming, or discuss generous behaviour towards animals as well as humans.

Buy good stuff. Less stuff made means less emissions and less climate damage. So buy high-quality things that last, repair broken items rather than throwing them out, buy and sell second-hand and borrow your neighbour's mower.

Dump less. Avoid excess packaging and buying pointless stuff that goes straight in the bin, recycle everything possible and compost your food waste if you can. Try to buy recycled whenever possible as well.

Don't waste food . . . The average British family throws away £50 worth of food every month. Use that good, old-fashioned thing a 'shopping list' to stop you buying quantities of 'offers' you don't need. Don't buy or cook more than you need and eat up those tasty leftovers.

. . . or water. Your tap water uses lots of energy, and heating it in your home uses loads more – so take showers rather than baths, be careful when watering plants and only run full dishwashers and washing machines. If you are still buying bottled water give yourself a sharp slap: you have been had by the marketing people.

Save the rainforest. Sign up with Cool Earth.
www.coolearth.org

Offset your emissions. However green or well-intentioned, we all use energy and produce carbon emissions when driving the car, heating our home or heading off on holiday. So pay for (offset) your carbon emissions by contributing an appropriate amount of money to a carbon-reducing environmental charity or project; planting trees or saving the rainforest. Various schemes and websites allow you to calculate your emissions, or if you're feeling courageous, check out your day-to-day carbon footprint on actonco2.direct.gov.uk and work out how to do something to reduce it.

10. My Generous Life

'To save one life is as if you have saved the world'

THE TALMUD

The steps I am going to take

This is not a 'self help' book, it is a 'help others' book. The purpose of writing it is to encourage everyone to live a more generous life, and to start doing so today, even if in only tiny ways.

So what are your first steps going to be? This is your chapter. A place for you to record what you have done or plan to do, the lives you have touched and the people who have touched yours.

Choose some of the 'First Steps' from the book that have inspired you (handily, they are repeated below) and decide what you are going to do about them. And then, rather than put it off, actually do something, and write it down. Note down, too, the generous things that have happened to you, the generous acts you have witnessed, the generous people you know, and generous things that you have done for other people, animals or even the planet.

Jot down your own ramblings about generosity and how you could or will live in a less acquisitive and more generous way – 'maximise your life, not your income' – and make your days more enjoyable and more worthwhile.

To help set you on your way, here are two stories (not originally intended for publication!) from people who saw the book before it was published. First from my friend Olly, who read the first draft:

'I thought you'd like to hear how the manuscript inspired me. Early the morning after reading it, I was heading down High Street Kensington on my way to work. Heading into Cafe Nero for my usual daily caffeine kick, I passed a man, huddled in his sleeping bag, in a storefront. As I was ordering my regular "Skinny Americano", I thought of what I had read the night before and changed the order, "actually can you make that two coffees please?". On the way out, I went up to the man and handed him a coffee. He looked at first astonished, then slightly baffled and finally realised that it was for him. He smiled and said "Thank you love. Appreciated". I walked to the bus stop with a bounce in my step; today was going to be a good day.'

Following Olly's example her husband George invited his secretary out to lunch for the first time ever. He emailed Olly "I asked my secretary out for lunch and I think she thinks I am behaving a little oddly!"

And this from John, the enormously patient, talented and good-looking editor of this book! (that's enough flattery, ed):

'I wonder if we should say more about the unexpected benefits of generosity, the way a simple act can create ripples well beyond the obvious. I think I told you yesterday that I had put stuff on Freecycle. One of the things was a CD/radio system on which the CD was not working. To be honest I felt a little guilty even giving it away – it was cheap and a bit rubbish. I said as much to the woman who came to pick it up. But she couldn't have been more happy. She was getting it for her autistic grandson, who loves fixing things. And Freecycle gives her the opportunity to find projects for him.'

As well as writing your thoughts here, you can also join our online community to contribute your ideas and stories:

www.pleasetakeonestep.com
www.facebook.com/pleasetakeonestep
www.twitter.com/pleasetakeone

Alternatively email me on

mikedickson@pleasetakeonestep.com

or write to me at

Please Take One
59A Portobello Road
London W11 3DB
UK.

First Steps: a reminder

What is Enough?

☐ Work out what is enough for you.

....

☐ Offest your lifestyle.

....

☐ Stop wasting food.

....

☐ Drink tapwater.

....

☐ Ask your local food stores what they do with their sur-
    plus stock.

....

☐ Maximise your life, not your income.

....

☐ Cook your own meals; don't buy ready-made.

....

☐ Buy presents that people actually want.

....

☐ Think before you shop: do you really need it?

....

☐ Tithe.

....

Notes

Combat Poverty

☐ Learn as much as you can about poverty in your own neighbourhood.

....

☐ Become a good listener.

....

☐ Throw a starfish back into the sea: make a difference, if only to one person.

....

☐ Resolve to offer practical support to those who are dealing with the most vulnerable and marginalised groups in our society.

....

☐ Sign up to 38 Degrees (**www.38degrees.org.uk**).

....

Notes

Help your Family and Friends

☐ Put some time aside in your diary to think about family and friends.

☐ Think about people at work.

☐ Cheer someone up.

☐ Be a Good Samaritan.

☐ Be secretly generous.

☐ Spread the work of The Kindness Offensive (**www.thekindnessoffensive.com**).

☐ Commit a Random Acts of Kindness.

☐ Join the organ donor register.

☐ Sign up to give blood.

☐ Let someone keep the change.

Notes

Help your Community

☐ Search out a local cause to support.

....

☐ Sign up to help the local environment.

....

☐ Help out at a local school.

....

☐ Provide community transport.

....

☐ Take someone shopping.

....

☐ Visit a hospital.

....

☐ Make a friend.

....

☐ Cook a meal and invite someone to share it.

....

☐ Make a home visit.

....

☐ Revamp that patch of waste ground.

....

☐ Join a committee.

....

Notes

Save the other world from poverty

☐ Keep an open mind.

....

☐ Learn the facts.

....

☐ Find out what works.

....

☐ Spend less of your holiday on the beach.

....

☐ Be the change, and fund a project.

....

☐ Twin your village, school or town.

....

☐ Help a friend with their project.

....

☐ Engage with an aid agency.

....

☐ Become a microfinancier.

....

Notes

Save the world's environment

☐ Become properly informed.

☐ Do no harm; institute a personal 'no net loss' programme.

☐ Fly less, holiday more.

☐ Save 10%: sign up to 10:10 (**www.1010.uk.org**).

☐ Drive less.

☐ Eat better, and have a meat-free day each week.

☐ Buy good stuff.

☐ Dump less.

☐ Don't waste food . . .

☐ . . . or water.

☐ Offset your emissions.

Notes

Resources

He who asks a question is a fool for a minute; he who does not remains a fool forever

CHINESE PROVERB.

The following books, articles and websites were inspirational to me in writing this book – if I've inspired you, there's plenty more reading here, along with websites and organisations who can help you start living a more generous life. Particular favourites are marked with a **.

1. The Age of I

Andrew Carnegie *The Gospel of Wealth* Carnegie's famous essay is widely available online. You can read more about the Carnegie Mellon founder and benefactor, and follow a link to the only known recording of his voice, as he reads some of his famous text, at **www.post-gazette.com/pg/07303/829537-28.stm.**

Charles Dickens *A Tale of Two Cities* Dickens has become a hero of mine. He wrote about and cared for the poor, and was one of the founders of what is now Great Ormond Street Hospital.

Bruce Feirstein's list of the 100 to Blame: **www.vanityfair.com/online/daily/2009/09/the-100-to-blame.html**

**Erich Fromm *To Have or To Be* Written in 1976 and even more relevant today. Fromm argues that we have a choice 'between a life based on selfishness and greed, or the other based on love, solidarity, creativity.'

E.F. Schumacher *Small is Beautiful* – *A Study of Economics as if People Mattered* Great book – does exactly what it says on the tin.

2. Generosity

Richard Dawkins *The Selfish Gene* And then there is our Generous Gene.

Nelson Mandela *Long Walk to Freedom* The great man's autobiography; inspiring and humbling.

Community Links A charity that helps disadvantaged local people, in a very effective way. David Robinson, the charity's founder, is an unassuming treasure trove of generous ideas. **www.community-links.org**

Disasters Emergency Committee An umbrella organisation which launches and coordinates responses to major disasters overseas like Haiti. **www.dec.org.uk**

Shakespeare and Company The website gives a good sense of the shop's ethos: if you are visiting Paris, be sure to drop in. **www.shakespeareandcompany.com**

3. Happiness

Stephen Covey and Roger Merrill *First Things First* 'The most important thing is, to keep the most important thing, the most important thing'. Stephen Covey's *Seven Habits of Highly Effective People* is also wonderful and should be on the school curriculum.

Elizabeth Dunn, Lara Aknin, Michael Norton *Spending Money on Others Promotes Happiness* An article, from Science journal March 2008, that demonstrates exactly what it says in the title.

**Viktor Frankl *Man's Search for Meaning* One of the most inspiring books on 'the purpose of life' ever written – a source for most self-help gurus.

Robert Holden Ph.D *Be Happy* An English happiness expert with a gentle sense of humour. www.happiness.co.uk

Sonja Lyubomirsky *The How of Happiness* Simple ways to lead a happier life. **www.chass.ucr.edu/faculty_book/lyubomirsky/**

Stephen G Post *Altruism, Happiness and Health: It's Good to be Good* International Journal of Behavioural Medicine 2005, Vol 12 N0 2, 66-77. Another powerful article with a self-explanatory title, demonstrating the power of altruism.

**Richard Schoch *The Secrets of Happiness* Three Thousand Years of Searching for the Good Life. One of my favourites!

Martin Seligman *Authentic Happiness* If you want to be happy be generous. If you want to learn about happiness, read Seligman. **www.authentichappiness.sas.upenn.edu**

4. Enough

**Charles Handy *The Elephant and the Flea* Another hero, great company, wise and wonderful. Credited with creating the concept of a Portfolio Life.

Oliver James *Affluenza* A really sensible observation, though the books could be shorter. From the same man who gave us *They F*** You Up: How to Survive Family Life* and controversial parenting advice in *How not to F*** Them Up*. Interesting, relevant, thoughtful writer.

Stuart Murray *Beyond Tithing* An intelligent book about the pros and cons of tithing. One of the cons being that people who give away 10% of their income think they've done enough.

John Naish *Enough: Breaking free from the world of more* Well written and thought provoking. **www.enoughness.co.uk**

Tristram Stuart *Waste: Uncovering the Global Food Scandal* Truly sobering and scarcely believable; this was one of the parts of my research that truly shocked me. **www.tristramstuart.co.uk

Leo Tolstoy *How Much Land Does A Man Need?* One of his most famous short stories, a parable about greed.

Catherine Walker & Cathy Pharoah *A Lot of Give: trends in charitable giving in the 21st century* Published by the Charities Aid Foundation, an examination of who gives what to whom. **www.cafonline.org**

Freecycle The good news is that it works. The bad news is, if you sign up, you need to be prepared for a deluge of emails. **www.freecycle.org**

Oxfam Inspired name for second-hand clothes – 'Loved for Longer'! Also does great work in very challenging worlds. **www.oxfam.org.uk**

5. Poverty in Britain

Age UK The new charity formed from a merger between Age Concern and Help the Aged. **www.ageuk.org.uk**

Chichester – the Big Love Association A small group of outlaws, trying to help homeless people living in the woods outside one of the wealthiest cities in the UK. Beyond parody. **www.biglove.org.uk**

Citizens Advice Bureau With offices all over the country, the CAB deals constantly with the poor and the scared. If you don't think poverty exists in this country, pop into one of their centres and speak to their volunteers. **www.citizensadvice.org.uk**

Fareshare A 'community food network', distributing surplus from the food industry to people who need it. See also the Trussel Trust. **www.fareshare.org.uk**

Ingeus Their goal is 'to help as many unemployed people as possible into jobs that will last'. Another growth business. **www.workdirections.co.uk**

The Poverty Site A great source of reliable statistics and facts about poverty in this country. **www.poverty.org.uk

The Trussel Trust A charity that feeds those who are hungry, and has a business plan to expand throughout Britain! **www.trusselltrust.org**

Unicef *Report Card 7, Child Poverty in Perspective: An Overview of Child Well-being in Rich Countries* An international report that should make us all hang our heads in shame. **www.unicef.org.uk/publications/pub_detail.asp?pub_id=124**

6. Generosity at Home

Max DePree *Leadership is an Art* The former CEO of Herman Miller writes simply about leadership from practical experience.

The Parable of the Good Samaritan Gospel of Luke, chapter 10, verses 25–37. Powerful wisdom from 2000 years ago.

Samaritans People who listen: an emotional support service for anyone in the UK and Ireland. **www.samaritans.org**

7. Generous communities

Charity Commission The body that oversees charities. If you are interested in finding out about a particular charity, this is a good place to begin. **www.charity-commission.gov.uk**

Donna's Dream House Where Gary met Barbara and Len and touched 3.4 million viewers. We need more Barbaras and Lens. And Garys. **www.donnasdreamhouse.co.uk**

Office for National Statistics A good source of up to date figures on the state of the Nation. **www.statistics.gov.uk

The Royal Borough of Windsor and Maidenhead A council ahead of its time, spearheading transparency in local government. **www.rbwm.gov.uk**

St Giles Trust Well run, award-winning charity that helps prisoners and re-offenders. **www.stgilestrust.org.uk**

Transition Towns An idea for the future, expanding now. **www.transitiontowns.org**

8. Global poverty

Paul Collier *The Bottom Billion – Why the Poorest Countries are Failing and what can be Done about it* A powerful, well written book outlining the links between war and poverty, the challenges of development agencies and questionable performance of governments. See also his *The Plundered Planet: How to Reconcile Prosperity with Nature*.

Dambisa Moyo *Dead Aid – Why aid is not working in Africa, and how there is another way for Africa* Ms Moyo's politically incorrect attack on the whole system of aid can make uncomfortable reading, especially as she clearly has a point.

Michael Norton *365 Ways to Change the World* The author is the creator of numerous NGOs, a one-man ideas factory, and charming with it! **www.365act.com**

Jacqueline Novogratz *The Blue Sweater – Bridging the Gap Between Rich and Poor in an Interconnected World* An inspiring book, written by a woman who went on to start the respected Acumen Fund. **www.acumenfund.org

Jeffrey Sachs *The End of Poverty – How We Can Make It Happen in Our Lifetime* Jeffrey Sachs, Director of The Earth Institute, argues convincingly that the world's problems are solvable. **www.earth.columbia.edu**

Peter Singer *The Life You Can Save – How to Play Your Part in Ending World Poverty* An Australian philosopher who argues that we can end world poverty and urges us to get on with it. Clear and straightforward arguments. Singer has also written about animal liberation.

A Glimmer of Hope If you are going to Ethiopia, or even if you are not, go and help them. They have also set up a UK charity helping young people. **www.aglimmerofhope.org**

I-India Charity doing wonderful work for street children in Jaipur; save a life for £35 per year! **www.i-indiaonline.com**

Shivia A small, growing microfinance NGO working in India and Nepal. For the price of your next meal out, a family can start a business and earn a sustainable income. Food for thought – literally! **www.shivia.com**

9. The Environment

Lester Brown *Plan B 4.0 – Mobilising to Save Civilisation* How to save the world, by the director of the Earth Policy Institute; read and learn. The book is available as a free download from their website. **www.earth-policy.org**

Jonathan Safran Foer *Eating Animals* Exploring a subject we'd rather not look at too closely, Foer makes a powerful case for becoming a vegetarian with his depictions of factory farms and their truly degrading conditions. And then there is the impact of eating meat on the environment. **www.eatinganimals.com

Felicity Lawrence *Not on the Label – What Really Goes Into the Food on Your Plate* Not so much the ingredients, as the exploitation and damage to the planet. If you were to stop and think about it, you probably would not eat much of what you do, so be warned – this may change your shopping habits for ever.

Carolyn Steel *Hungry City* How much food it takes to feed a city; never mind every city. **www.hungrycitybook.co.uk**

10:10 Remarkable 'can do' organisation that has revolutionised the communication about the challenges to our environment. **www.1010uk.org

Age of Stupid Film with a futuristic take on what the world might be like in 2050. What is left of it. **www.ageofstupid.net**

End of the Line A great film, well made and a real, if grim, education. Everything you ever wanted to know about fishing (and more) but didn't dare ask. **www.endoftheline.com

Extreme Ice Survey The brainchild of James Balog (see p.162), a remarkable man doing remarkable work. **www.extremeicesurvey.org**

Friends of the Earth Environmental campaign group active in the UK and worldwide. Their website is a rich source of articles on climate change, the rainforest, palm oil and more. **www.foe.co.uk**

Greenpeace Worldwide campaigning organisation whose website has vast amounts of information about the issues facing the planet, including palm oil, fishing and the rainforest. **www.greenpeace.org.uk**

Livestock's Long Shadow Jointly published by LEAD (Livestock, Environment and Development) and the FAO (the UN Food and Agriculture Organisation), this is a sobering take on a little known contributor to our environmental challenges. Download it from the FAO website. **www.fao.org**

No Net Loss The Business and Biodiversity Offsets Programme (BBOP) is a high-level group working with governments and business on the principles of no net loss or, better still, net positive impact. **http://bbop.forest-trends.org**

Ted Ideas worth spreading – clever, inspiring and funny talks by extraordinary people given at Ted conferences and available online. Brain food on your laptop or iPhone. **www.ted.com

The Author

Mike Dickson advises companies on how to develop effective and inspiring relationships with charities. Partnerships which make business sense, inspire employees and help to create a more intelligent business. He has recently advised on the successful creation of two new charitable foundations for Bridgepoint, a leading private equity firm, and White Stuff, the fast-growing fashion retailer. He also advises individuals and families on their private philanthropy.

Mike co-founded the successful children's charity Whizz-Kidz, which provides mobility equipment for disabled children. Whizz-Kidz is the largest UK supplier of paediatric mobility aids outside the NHS, and has raised over £50 million to provide equipment for more than 7,500 children and young people.

Mike writes regular columns about philanthropy for the Business Spectator. He is also the author of The More You Give, The More You Get, which explains how both individuals and companies can give effectively, and how the charity world works.

Mike has 'been round six marathons', led fundraising treks in the Himalayas and Peru, is married with two children and lives in West London. He is a church warden of St Peter's Church, Notting Hill Gate.

www.themoreyougive.co.uk

www.whizz-kidz.org.uk

www.pleasetakeonestep.com